MADV[...]

Praise for the series

It was only a matter of time before a clever publisher realized that there is an audience for whom *Exile on Main Street* or *Electric Ladyland* are as significant and worthy of study as *The Catcher in the Rye* or *Middlemarch* ... The series ... is freewheeling and eclectic, ranging from minute rock-geek analysis to idiosyncratic personal celebration — *The New York Times Book Review*

Ideal for the rock geek who thinks liner notes just aren't enough
— *Rolling Stone*

One of the coolest publishing imprints on the planet — *Bookslut*

These are for the insane collectors out there who appreciate fantastic design, well-executed thinking, and things that make your house look cool. Each volume in this series takes a seminal album and breaks it down in startling minutiae. We love these. We are huge nerds — *Vice*

A brilliant series ... each one a work of real love — *NME (UK)*

Passionate, obsessive, and smart — *Nylon*

Religious tracts for the rock 'n' roll faithful — *Boldtype*

[A] consistently excellent series — *Uncut* (UK)

We ... aren't naive enough to think that we're your only source for reading about music (but if we had our way ... watch out). For those of you who really like to know everything there is to know about an album, you'd do well to check out Bloomsbury's "33 1/3" series of books — *Pitchfork*

For almost 20 years, the 33-and-a-Third series of music books has focused on individual albums by acts well known (Bob Dylan, Nirvana, Abba, Radiohead), cultish (Neutral Milk Hotel, Throbbing Gristle, Wire) and many levels in-between. The range of music and their creators defines "eclectic", while the writing veers from freewheeling to acutely insightful. In essence, the books are for the music fan who (as Rolling Stone noted) "thinks liner notes just aren't enough" — *The Irish Times*

For reviews of individual titles in the series, please visit our blog at 333sound.com and our website at https://www.bloomsbury.com/uk/ academic/music-sound-studies/

Follow us on Twitter: @333books

Like us on Facebook: https://www.facebook.com/33.3books

For a complete list of books in this series, see the back of this book.

Forthcoming in the series:

and many more …

Madvillainy

Will Hagle

BLOOMSBURY ACADEMIC
NEW YORK • LONDON • OXFORD • NEW DELHI • SYDNEY

BLOOMSBURY ACADEMIC
Bloomsbury Publishing Inc
1385 Broadway, New York, NY 10018, USA
50 Bedford Square, London, WC1B 3DP, UK
29 Earlsfort Terrace, Dublin 2, Ireland

BLOOMSBURY, BLOOMSBURY ACADEMIC and the Diana logo
are trademarks of Bloomsbury Publishing Plc

First published in the United States of America 2023
Reprinted 2023 (four times), 2024 (twice)

Library of Congress Cataloging-in-Publication Data
Names: Hagle, Will, author.
Title: Madvillainy / Will Hagle.
Description: New York : Bloomsbury Academic, 2023. |
Series: 33 1/3 | Includes bibliographical references. |
Summary: "Unpacks the complex layers of Madvillainy, the 2004 classic
collaborative LP between producer Madlib and rapper MF DOOM, whose
success both relied on and rejected the tendencies of the
social media age"– Provided by publisher.
Identifiers: LCCN 2022042742 (print) | LCCN 2022042743 (ebook) |
ISBN 9781501389238 (paperback) | ISBN 9781501389245 (epub) |
ISBN 9781501389252 (pdf) | ISBN 9781501389269 (ebook other)
Subjects: LCSH: Madvillain (Musical group). Madvillainy. | Madlib, 1973- |
MF Doom. | Rap (Music)–2001-2010–History and criticism.
Classification: LCC ML421.M324 H34 2023 (print) |
LCC ML421.M324 (ebook) | DDC 782.421649092/2–dc23/eng/20220914
LC record available at https://lccn.loc.gov/2022042742
LC ebook record available at https://lccn.loc.gov/2022042743

ISBN: PB: 978-1-5013-8923-8
          ePDF: 978-1-5013-8925-2
          eBook: 978-1-5013-8924-5

Series: 33 1/3

Typeset by Integra Software Services Pvt. Ltd.
Printed and bound in Great Britain

To find out more about our authors and books visit
www.bloomsbury.com and sign up for our newsletters.

Contents

Greetings. Self's name: Timothy A.I. Verselli, sentient computer program and the last remaining employee of *The Daily Daily*'s Music Journalism department.

TASK: To compile and present to you, human reader, this collection of articles pertaining to the topic of:

[…]

Madvillainy.

[…]

Before beginning, allow Self to auto-generate an intro article.

TASK: To explain how this book came together, and what you can expect from it, emulating Madvillain's model of using fiction to hint at the Truth.

[…]

The Daily Daily vs. Music Journalism

The Editor schedules an emergency meeting. Calls *The Daily Daily*'s entire Music Journalism department into her office.

Dr. Truthaverse arrives on time, says, "Sorry I'm late. What's this about?"

The Editor is a silhouette against a wall-length window, the sun obscuring her but illuminating Manhattan.

"New assignment. From upstairs," The Editor says. "The story of Madvillain."

Twenty-two Music Journalists GASP in dissonant unison.

"But … they're … … mysterious villains," one offers. "Can't we just leave them alone?"

The Editor's fist SLAMS into the window.

"SILENCE! *Madvillainy*'s 20th anniversary is coming up. The data suggests that if we time this right, our department can climb back out of the red. But if we don't produce our MOST-CLICKED articles EVER, we'll all be packing our belongings and heading back … " The Editor says, then pauses to point her silhouetted thumb behind her. "Out there … "

A pigeon SQUAWKS and THUDS to a sudden silence against the transparent pane, sliding down with a slow squeak, leaving behind a bloody stream. The Music

Journalists shudder and grumble on an off-kilter delay from each other and the rattling window-walls.

"Wow. I didn't plan that," The Editor says. "Speaking of planning, we need to plan these assignments. Dr. Truthaverse, you tell blatant sarcastic lies as a convoluted way of conveying the actual truth, right?"

Dr. Truthaverse takes a slow sip from his empty mug.

" … No? My article titled 'Why David Axelrod Was Not An Underrated Influential Musician' definitely was not one of the Top-Clicked articles this fiscal quarter."

" … Okay, well, the bosses upstairs think an article exposing the truth of MF DOOM and his role in Madvillain could be a big hit. Research reports that 99% of existing articles about DOOM are inaccurate. We want to tell the truest story ever. Can you do that?"

"Nope!"

"Great, I think. Thanks." The Editor says, then points at her open laptop and asks, "Hey The Seen, are you on?"

The rustling friction of a hand against a microphone sputters out of the speaker. The Seen, joining via video conference from Southern California, clears his throat.

"Yeah sorry I was muted. And my camera's still not turning on for some reason … Hang on. Did that work?"

"No, we can't see you. Which is exactly my point. No one ever knows where you are. Except when your camera did turn on that one time, but you weren't in front of it, so we didn't see where you were but we unfortunately did hear that you were in the bathroom."

Twenty-two Music Journalists CHUCKLE in amused reminiscent harmony.

"Madlib is an elusive artist. Maybe you can understand. Track him down and write his backstory."

"There we go, now you should be able to see me. What were you sa—"

The Editor SLAMS her laptop shut.

"Alright, let's start with those two articles. We just need some backstory. Context. If they perform well, we'll get into the story of how DOOM and Madlib came together as Madvillain, and recorded *Madvillainy*: an album which straddled the analog and digital eras while exceeding expectations in both. How it leaked onto the internet, and spread among a network of global fans, then came out in altered form in 2004 on Stones Throw Records, and changed independent hip-hop, and then mainstream music, forever."

The Editor takes a step forward. Opens her eyes into the room's harsh fluorescent glow, which now illuminates her un-silhouetted body. Realizes that everyone except Dr. Truthaverse and a random intern scattered back to their desks during her impassioned rant.

"Maybe then we can get into how the album is much more than a collection of songs," says the random intern. "How it's a folkloric artifact that's spawned infinite legends. How *Madvillainy*, like DOOM and Madlib, has always been bigger than itself."

The Editor pauses, considers, shrugs, says, "Eh. I don't know."

The random intern, with misguided confidence, asks, "If this series of articles ever becomes a book, can I at least write the preface?"

"Sure, kid. If that happens, we'll even slap your name on the cover," The Editor says with a dismissive laugh. "For now, leave the writing to a veteran like Dr. Truthaverse."

"Sounds good! I'll get right on it," Dr. Truthaverse says, throwing his mug in the trash and moving toward the door.

"Dr. Truthaverse, wait!" The Editor says, stepping in front of him, lowering her voice to a whisper. "The bosses upstairs are hounding me for an update. You're still coding that program, right? The artificially intelligent journalist?"

Dr. Truthaverse's neck creaks as he rotates his head slowly from side to side.

Preface

By Will Hagle

This book, like *Madvillainy*, is a work of fiction.

In homage to *Madvillainy*, in which Daniel Dumile and Otis Jackson Jr. appear under multiple aliases, I write from alternating perspectives of three music journalists who work for a fake publication called *The Daily Daily*. There are also un-illustrated comics about the characters as interludes between chapters.

Dr. Truthaverse, The Seen, and Timothy A.I. Verselli had nothing to do with the creation of *Madvillainy* and neither did I. Several people who were involved in some form, excluding the actual two artists and several other understandably reluctant individuals, did share with me many stories, facts, and opinions. Before our interviews, I explained that I am just a fan who wants to celebrate DOOM, Madlib, and Madvillain's eternal unknowability. To tell my own specific rendition of an endlessly-interpretable story, hindered like all accounts by secondhand knowledge, inescapable biases, and a word count limit.

This book attempts to honor DOOM and Madlib's intentional aversion to Truth, focusing instead on what I refer to as Falsehood: the unverifiable legends that attracted and activated the artists' combined and respective fan bases, creating a folklore that perpetuates the significance of their collaborative project. As long as we keep listening to *Madvillainy*, and passing on stories about the artists who mean so much to so many of us, that legend will live on.

Laundromat.

MF DOOM

DR. TRUTHAVERSE VS. THE SUPERVILLAIN

By Dr. Truthaverse

No biographer—especially moi, your friendly neighborhood Dr. Truthaverse—could document DOOM's life with any degree of certitude. You could say he was born Daniel Dumile, in 1971, in Hounslow, a suburban area of West London.[1] The first in a series of origin stories, each of which led to unintended consequences. In the case of his UK birth, the long-term outcome was Dumile's 2010 deportation from and denial of re-entry to the United States, where he grew up. A banishment that continued through the end of his life and revealed, to his family, friends, and global network of adoring fans, the tragic Truth of the American immigration system. This led to him resettling in London, and later St. Lucia, Grenada, or an unspecified Caribbean island to throw off his detective-like fan base, without explanation, and then booking shows in the United States and sending semi-obvious DOOMposters to lip-synch from behind a mask. One of the many ways in which Dumile responded to pain and inequity with resilient but frustrating humor. In signature villainous fashion, DOOM somehow both enraged and delighted.

You could say the Dumile family moved through multiple New York locations before settling on Long Island, in Long Beach. A seaside suburban community an hour-long straight shot on the LIRR from Penn Station. Easy access to neighboring Queens or Brooklyn, but not quite "the city."

You could say this and someone could say you're wrong and who are you to say that anyways? As a public figure, Dumile constructed an elaborate missile defense system around himself to intercept the media and fans' relentless intrusive projectiles. Post-transition, those closest to him strive to protect the mysteriousness that he cultivated in the physical realm. They protect his legacy like the Swiss Guard does the Pope: independent defenders of an infallible figure.

Dumile cultivated his own mythology with meticulous intentional effort. By the time *Madvillainy* came out on Stones Throw in 2004, he had released a record as King Geedorah on the label Big Dada/Ninja Tune, and another as Viktor Vaughn on Sound Ink Records. MF DOOM's *MM..FOOD* came out on Rhymesayers the same year as *Madvillainy*. These multiple monikers added a protective layer between Dumile and his music.

Although most MCs have alter egos, often based on comics or superheroes, the DOOMiverse is expansive and evolving, with interwoven characters and subplots. MF DOOM is a mask-wearing supervillain modeled after Marvel's Dr. Doom. King Geedorah, like the nemesis monster from

Godzilla, is a three-headed lizard who channels the beats he makes from outer space. Viktor Vaughn is the younger version of DOOM, a "rapper-for-hire" who writes and recites bars only if the checks clear. Commitment to this latter bit resulted in Viktor rapping for what a superfan on a forum calculated to be a total of nine minutes and thirty seconds out of the 32:53 runtime on his second album *VV:2*.[2]

Dumile hints at the distinct quirks of his characters without overt exposition. He raps in similes and punch lines, not a narrative style. The storytelling happens later, in the minds of fans who hear his music, interpret it, and interact with each other. Because DOOM hides behind a mask, and infuses his work with cryptic flashes of world-building detail, appreciating his art to its fullest extent requires a more active form of participation. First-time listeners to *Madvillainy*, devoid of insight or context, might miss several jokes or details even if the overall tone or specific lines resonate.

You could play *Madvillainy* every day and discover new meaning in specific diction. It's not surprising that DOOM idolized Charles Bukowski, who wrote with blunt, terse prose, but included lines that could be arresting in their dense profundity. Dumile, too, calls himself a writer. DOOM, like King Geedorah or Viktor Vaughn, is one character who contains aspects of the author's real life, like Bukowski's Hank Chinaski.

Dumile appeared in public most often how he looks on *Madvillainy's* album art: as DOOM, with his face obscured behind a mask. Part of Dumile's admitted intention behind DOOM's mask was to emphasize the importance of musical and lyrical ability over showy possessions or flashy appearance. DOOM calls himself ugly on *MM..FOOD*'s "Beef Rapp," but the mask was more than defense against vanity. Like the supervillain he molded himself into, Dumile reveled in anonymity, happily slipping undetected through crowds of cheering fans after shows.

Dumile's hidden face also had the opposite of his intended effect. The mask became a unique form of flashy appearance. The bosses at *The Daily Daily*, like hordes of nosy fans, are desperate to unmask DOOM and See Dumile's Truth. But Dumile the author cannot be known.

When I reached out to interview Bobbito Garcia—exalted DJ and founder of Fondle 'Em, the label which first released Dumile's debut LP as MF DOOM, *Operation: DOOMsday*—he declined. His rejection, which matches the responses of several others, is sensical and understandable. Of course this topic is emotionally draining. Dumile was Bobbito's friend. You can hear Bobbito laughing at the end of "Rhymes Like Dimes," which DOOM recorded in his bedroom. Instead of closing with a verse or another hook at the end of the beat, DOOM handed Bobbito a microphone and told him to talk. Bobbito said whatever wild combination of words came to his mind—including stopping to ask what, exactly, people are supposed to say at the end of records—before sitting in the uncomfortable moment of DOOM not responding, and continuing on with more hilarious free association. DOOM left the raw recording on the finished track, not caring that Bobbito bumped the mic out of excitement and left an audible peak.[3] That is an incredible moment on a record that's been immortalized in hip-hop history, but to Bobbito and DOOM it's a real memory. The specifics of some legends are better left contained within the brains of those that spawned them.

Because DOOM guarded his personal identity, stories like these aren't just about him. They *are* him. DOOM is a conglomeration of unsubstantiated ideas, rumors, and anecdotes. A tall tale involving chaotic DOOM antics coincides with every point in his career, through his death in 2020 at age 49: announced on New Year's Eve via social media two months after his Halloween passing, which the most conspiracy-minded believe *must be* an elaborate hoax.

I will never be able to encapsulate the Truth of what moments like Bobbito's freestyle'd session meant to the people closest to DOOM in the lead up to *Madvillainy*. Like moi, DOOM's mission is to redirect you away from the Truth and toward a Falsehood of his own construction. A Falsehood that grew more legendary leading up to *Madvillainy*, multiplied over the decades following the album's release, and will outlast Dumile's physical existence, now that the masses have taken hold.

The first legend a *Madvillainy* listener needs to know is a symbolic tale of tragic loss and resilient resurgence. A quintessential piece of hip-hop mythology: DOOM's origin story. A Falsehood I left the Midtown Manhattan office to investigate.

BUT FIRST!: DR. TRUTHAVERSE'S ORIGIN STORY

By Timothy A.I. Verselli

Six-year-old Timothy A. Verselli slips and falls into the sewer of boiling Truth.

WHEEEEEEEEEEW!

In his scant years leading up to the incident, Timothy lived in an age-appropriate world of imagination. He'd hover over the unhinged pothole cover in the alley behind his Brooklyn brownstone, mind conjuring what might lie beneath: dragons, elves, monsters? Anything could be lurking in those uncertain depths, because Timothy's purity had been protected through Falsehood: the shielded world adults construct for children and themselves. The fabricated world where the Tooth Fairy theoretically exists, even if she never visits. Where brothers and fathers and sons live forever. A world which, without fail, falls apart at some point for every growing individual, at differing intervals and with varying degrees of shock and intensity.

For Timothy it happens at once. When he plops into the sewer of boiling Truth, society's Falsehood shatters into irreparable pieces.

POW!

Right in the kisser: the cold asexual lips of unfiltered reality. Timothy feels no physical pain as the Truth burns through his skin. But he experiences incomprehensible anguish.

The average human confronts a fraction of the Truth over the course of a lifetime spent running from it. Timothy ingests it all in an instant.

When he re-emerges, excess Truth serum oozing onto the wet concrete, he looks like the same unscathed young boy. But when he hears his father's voice calling out, "Timothy! Timothy?", he doesn't respond. Turns and walks the other direction. Timothy no longer exists. Now he is Dr. Truthaverse. Where can he find a mask and a cape?

Twenty Years Later:

Dr. Truthaverse's body has grown to match his burdened spirit. He refers to his potbelly as a six-pack, and his unkempt splotches of facial hair as his beard. Inaccuracy is, in his adult life, what brings him an approximation of pleasure. Dr. Truthaverse seeks out Falsehood: attends weddings, religious ceremonies, and gatherings of so-called friends. Patrols the streets, protecting the masses from Truth. Distracts one spouse while the other sneaks out with a lover. Snaps in people's faces and points down, urging them to return their close yet distant gaze to their screens. Reassures nieces and nephews that their doggy is happier now at the great farm in the sky.

But Dr. Truthaverse can't fool himself. Being a self-avowed superhero doesn't pay the bills. He scans the classifieds:

MADVILLAIN BISTRO BED & BREAKFAST BAR & GRILL CAFE LOUNGE

NOW HIRING:

COOK

No. Dr. Truthaverse can't be a cook. Recipes are too literal. Food, too predictable. Restaurant workers too real.

If Dr. Truthaverse has to work forty hours per week, his job needs to be filled with Falsehood. With inflated egos and clout-seeking frauds. Fiction is tolerable. Truth is unbearable.

Scrolling his finger down the listings, he stops and taps his finger on the one career that matches his criteria.

THE DAILY DAILY
NOW HIRING:
MUSIC JOURNALIST

ESCAPE FROM LONG ISLAND

By Dr. Truthaverse

The train screeches to a halt. *Last stop, Long Beach station.* Stepping off onto the platform, I exhale visible breath into the cold air. One car rolls through a freshly green stoplight. A few pedestrians amble past a Philadelphia Pretzel Factory, a sushi shop and a Mexican cantina: today's businesses able to afford rent on the suburb's short main thoroughfare. Nearby is the Long Beach boardwalk, where a young Dumile and his b-boy peers would spend time breaking. The morning's dense fog makes the sea unseeable but I know, instinctively, that it is there. Much like Dumile's childhood. The villain did grow up in this neighborhood, but New York continues consuming itself, regurgitating its graffiti-bombed faces in altered forms. I am here to investigate DOOM's origin story, but I should have stayed at my desk. Whatever Long Beach looked like in Dumile's adolescence must have been morphing more rapidly in each year of his absence.

A few buildings crucial to Dumile's upbringing still stand. The first is the house where Dumile and his siblings grew up. Less than two blocks away is the Martin Luther King Community Center, a formative gathering point for Long Beach residents today and during Dumile's childhood.

"The Martin Luther King Center, one of the congregating areas for many people in the community, was created out of the civil rights and Black Power movements. Many Southern migrants were involved with that. In the whole area of Long

Beach, there was already a sense of Black pride. Definitely a sense of community, and owning one's own community," says Dr. Graham, a civil rights and social justice leader who attended high school with Dumile.

While demographics and businesses have changed, Long Beach's communal spirit has not. Dumile's onetime presence, too, lingers. Dr. Graham helped push the city to designate East Hudson St. between Riverside and Long Beach Rd.— the block where the Dumiles grew up—as the honorary "KMD/MF DOOM Way." The street sign memorializes the soil that sprouted a globally impactful artist. Some slight recognition in a country which, rather than accepting him as a homegrown hero, banished DOOM, like a villain, forever.

"The city of Long Beach got it right, but the American immigration system got it wrong," Dr. Graham said in his speech at the dedication ceremony, and repeats to me during our interview.[4]

On KMD/MF DOOM Way, the houses are expansive, with porches and yards. You could fit most of Manhattan's street-tossed trash in the open green spaces between units. In the 1980s, DOOM's teenage lair had a unique gravitational pull, the way the steaming pothole behind my Brooklyn brownstone lured me in. Most former children can recall a similar situation: one house in the neighborhood becomes the center of the universe. Daniel and his younger brother Dingilizwe hung out there together throughout their teenage years along with their crew: the Get Yours Posse, or the GYP.

The GYP embedded themselves in the expanding cultural movement of hip-hop, which had literally grown up with them. DJ Kool Herc's infamous Bronx block party, regarded as hip-hop's mythological origin, happened two years after Dumile's birth. Artists like Rakim and Erick Sermon ensured that Long Island was distant only in train travel time from the epicenter of New York City's exploding musicality in the mid- to late-1980s.

The Dumile brothers would write graffiti, b-boy, make beats, DJ, MC. They were swept up in the movement, on the precipice of ushering in its Golden Age. In high school, they formed a group called KMD with their friend Rodan, who Onyx the Birthstone Kid soon replaced. The initials, which they chose with graffiti aesthetic in mind,[5] stood for "Kausing Much Damage." A shift in perspective inspired them to change this to "a positive Kause in a Much Damaged society."

Growing up, those closest to the future MF DOOM already called him "Doom," a riff on the pronunciation of his last name: *Doom-i-lay*. In KMD, he was "Zev Love X." Read backwards, the name says, "X evoLveZ," a nod to Malcolm X.[6] Zev and Dingilizwe, AKA DJ Subroc, were members of the Ansaaru Allah community: a branch of the Five Percent Nation that studied under Dr. Malachai York. They spent weekends studying at headquarters in Bushwick or at Dr. York's compound upstate. Their lyrics and aesthetic reflected their ideology, much like other groups with Five Percent influence, including future labelmates Brand Nubian and Leaders of the New School.

KMD were teenagers who loved comic books, skateboarding, movies, literature, music and hanging out, who also wanted to enlighten themselves and others. Zev's lyrics, while youthful and fun, had a political perspective. The group had an unabashed intent of speaking Truth to America's unbalanced power structure, and shedding light on ignored or oppressed ideas and teachers.

"Black and Latinx migrants, who carry a lot of the same culture, birthed hip-hop. Whether it was blues, jazz, or gospel. There's a lot of people who attended churches, and also had their toe in the street. So [KMD] took a lot of what Black culture had to offer and made it part of their everyday existence," says Dr. Graham.

I always thought it was interesting that I could be listening to A Tribe Called Quest and eating grits at the same time. Because it was part of the merging of Black culture in this one place. [KMD] was privy to that, along with the influences of Allah, the resurrection of a Black thought and Black pride, particularly in the late '80s. So, you have also Islamic influence with them, and the Five Percent Nation growing at that time. There's a lot of different influences that they see, experience, become part of and help actually build. Looking back on it and contextualizing, I think there's a level of multiple factors that are influencing their existence.

At one fortuitous local talent show, Daniel Dumile met Michael Berrin, who lived in neighboring Far Rockaway and rapped under the name MC Serch. Like the Dumiles, Serch had started a hip-hop trio, teaming with Brooklyn-raised DJ Richie Rich and Columbia student Pete Nice under the name 3rd Bass. Serch became part of the GYP, forming a genuine bond with Zev and making consistent treks to hang out at the

Dumile house.[7] After some of Serch's singles, like "Hey Boy," became regional hits, 3rd Bass signed a deal with Def Jam.

Loyal to the GYP, 3rd Bass enlisted Zev Love X for a guest verse on what would become their biggest single from 1991's *The Cactus Album*, an inescapable record produced by Prince Paul called "The Gas Face." In the song's opening verse, Pete Nice gives credit to Zev Love X for inventing its namesake's now-iconic gesture. In the video, a young Dumile sticks out his tongue and shakes his head, demonstrating the goofily expressed symbol of disgust and disrespect. "The Gas Face" hit number five on the Billboard Rap Singles charts in 1990. 3rd Bass brought DOOM on tour and on Arsenio Hall to perform his verse.

During the rapid-fire shout outs at the end of the song, the group gives a joking gas face to A&R executive Dante Ross. KMD must not have harbored any True ill feelings toward Ross, who soon signed the group to Elektra Records: Dumile's first and most legitimate deal. By 1990 KMD had begun working on what would become their debut LP, *Mr. Hood*.

Both Dumile brothers were involved in the album's production, which they sequenced on a Casio FZ-1. Like all brothers they differed in personality and work ethic, but their respective approaches to beatmaking completed each other. Daniel was less regimented and serious, possessing a looseness that would appeal to fans in his later-in-life resurgence. At times, as DOOM, Dumile raps off-beat, or leaves obvious imperfections like the aforementioned Bobbito mic bump. *Mr. Hood* by comparison, is tightly woven.

"Sub was more of the scientist. The technician," says Dante Ross. "DOOM is a little haphazard and spontaneous with production. Which lends to his charm. But the KMD record is pretty intricate. Sub was more involved in the production than DOOM was. DOOM would start a lot of stuff, and Sub would finish it."

The album laid the foundation for a career in which Dumile would approach each project from a high-concept perspective. Mr. Hood is the name of a character who appears across interspersed skits, talking in an uncanny voice to KMD members, who enlighten him, and the listener, over the course of the album. In an interview with RBMA from 2015, DOOM revealed that Mr. Hood's vocal lines were stitched together from a Spanish language instructional vinyl.[8] The Dumile brothers sampled phrases that the instructor said in English, and rearranged them into new sentences. This signature approach—indebted in part to Prince Paul and other contemporaries—characterized DOOM's production style, and resurfaced with Madlib's assistance on *Madvillainy*. The Dumile brothers built cohesive collages out of disparate fragments, sampling and rearranging spoken sentences like they're drums or horns.

"Peachfuzz," the LP's single, climbed to #11 on 1991's Billboard Rap Singles chart.[9] KMD didn't become overnight household names, but *Mr. Hood* launched them on an upward trajectory, and a tour with labelmates Brand Nubian, Pete Rock & CL Smooth, and Leaders of the New School. The album sold enough copies to recoup its initial investment and allow KMD to begin recording a follow-up, which the trio spent the next year and a half working on.

About a year before their sophomore LP's May 1994 scheduled release, tragedy struck. On April 23, 1993, Subroc left the rapper Cage's place in upper Manhattan, where he'd hung out and spent the night, then took the train back to Long Island.[10] While attempting to cross the Long Island Expressway on foot, a vehicle hit and killed him. In the grief-ridden days following Subroc's death, rumors swirled about specifics. In a June 1994 interview in *The Source*, Zev calls the incident "shady."[11] Details about the cause of the accident are hazy, but the outcome is clear. In the midst of KMD's rise, a crucial member transitioned out of this realm. DOOM lost his spiritual twin, his musical counterpart, his brother.

Of the many tales spun out of this sad time in Dumile's life, one stands out for its heartbreaking symbolism. At the funeral, DOOM allegedly placed a boombox in front of the coffin and played back the unfinished tracks from the forthcoming album, *Black Bastards*.[12] The best way for Dumile to honor Subroc's legacy would be to make their music heard.

> We buried Sub, which was completely ridiculously emotional for all of us. Far more so for DOOM, obviously. DOOM fell back for a minute. I remember talking to him, and I was like "What do you want to do?" He was like, "I want to finish the record." Almost like, "Why would you even ask me that? Of course I'm finishing my record,"

says Ross.

Anyone who heard *Black Bastards*, either at the time or much later, regarded it as an improvement over *Mr. Hood*. The follow-up is more foreboding than the predecessor. It opens with another collage of establishing vocal clips, devoid of the first LP's playfulness and upbeat energy. The Dumile brothers took inspiration from Last Poet founding member Gylan Kain's 1970 album *The Blue Guerrilla*, a prominent sample, which features spoken word poetry pertaining to the racial injustices of America over an intense jazz soundtrack. KMD had grown up and refined their sound. They'd become more complete artists, both clearer in their exploration of values and topics most important to them and more determined to stick to their guiding principles. In the aforementioned interview in *The Source*, a couple of months removed from his brother's death, Zev Love X implied that *Black Bastards* was Truer to the music they made before Serch and others in the industry meddled with their creative direction by guiding them toward crossover appeal.

Soon before the album's scheduled release, however, Ross had to deliver DOOM more unfortunate news: Elektra had shelved *Black Bastards*, and dropped KMD from their roster.

In retrospect, the justification for the album's shelving makes no sense. The official reason was that the album artwork, which DOOM had drawn, was offensive and therefore too risky an investment. On the cover, DOOM depicts a sketch of a common racist caricature being hung from a noose like the game Hangman. The album's title appears below, with a few letters missing. Repurposing Sambo had been a long-standing theme of KMD's iconography. The meaning isn't difficult to decode. White America belittled Black people through racist cartoons over centuries of violent oppression. KMD rejected that. From the label's perspective,

Ice T's "Cop Killer" set off a wave of controversy a year prior. The financial implications for their parent company, Warner Bros., were dire. Elektra feared comparable blowback. No matter how hard Ross fought for his artists' freedom of expression, the label finalized the decision.

"It was, and it remains, the biggest injustice I've ever personally been in the middle of in the entire record business. I've done this for years, so I've seen a bunch of bullshit. But that, to me, was the biggest travesty of justice I'd ever seen and just completely an unrighteous act," says Ross.

The only thing left for Dumile to do was walk away. So he did.

Dumile receding from the major label music industry is the cliffhanger at the end of this chapter in DOOM's origin story. In re-tellings of his legend, most cite Subroc's death and Elektra dropping KMD as the cataclysmic sequence of events which led to the formation of our villain. Like Dr. Victor Von Doom scarring his face with irreversible burns in a failed attempt to resurrect his deceased mother.

This moment also marks the beginning of Dumile's life taking on folkloric qualities. Because record stores, magazines, and radio stations had received test pressings of *Black Bastards*, the album circulated via bootlegged copies. The legend of what happened to KMD spread.

"The mainstream story was Ice T's 'Cop Killer,' but the underground story was what happened to KMD," says the photographer and filmmaker B+.

"[*Black Bastards*] was real folklorish," says J. Rocc, a DJ who's worked closely with DOOM and Madlib. "Like, KMD got dropped, and their album is so controversial, and it's never going to come out! That was a big mysterious thing for that time."

For several years after *Black Bastards*' shelving, DOOM disappeared. Lived on friends' couches. If he recorded music, he had no intention of releasing it.

No one knows more intimately than moi—your friendly neighborhood Dr. Truthaverse—what it's like to be lonely in New York. After arriving to investigate my subject, I leave Long Beach within an hour, spending less time in Dumile's hometown than the train from Midtown took to get there. Aside from the street sign, there is nothing there that will bring me closer to his Truth.

I return to Penn Station and walk for miles past thousands of faces that don't acknowledge my presence. I am a ghost, like Dumile was and is. Moving through. Parents push their children on strollers. Dogs pee on fire hydrants. Rats scurry through trash piles. Two people sit on a stoop and pass a flask back and forth. A couple yells at each other. Another holds hands. Kisses. Somewhere in the city a baby is born and a grandmother dies. The world continues spinning, much like it did in KMD's absence. When the industry finished with Dumile it spat him out, like I do a lugee onto the sidewalk. A thousand soles will walk over my dried saliva in the course of an afternoon, remnants of my DNA seeping into their socks with holes, and none of them will know I existed. Life carried on this way throughout the mid-90s for Zev Love X, who the masses began to forget. Daniel Dumile faded into the city, another insignificant face in the ever-shifting concrete sea.

And then, when no one was asking for him, he put on a mask and returned.

'Til He's Back Where We All Go

In his years away from the industry, Dumile didn't hibernate in total isolation. He hung around an active community of artists, graffiti writers, DJs, radio hosts, producers, rappers, and independent label executives. An uptown crew called the CM, or Criminal Minded, or Constipated Monkeys. Some friends were essential for his literal and spiritual survival, providing shelter, financial support, and musical equipment. Most of these people made the Truth of their email addresses or phone numbers too difficult even for this music journalist slash superhero to track down.

Perhaps it's best to leave the years after Subroc's passing as a blank slate of uncertainty. That enhances the significance of what happened next: Dumile did pick the microphone back up. Held it in his hand in Bobbito's bedroom and let the words pour out. No need to bother with a real studio. The industry had banished him, and after his forced absence, he returned for independent vengeance.

When Dumile rapped again around 1997, he didn't call himself Zev Love X. He conceptualized a new character, inspired by the Jack Kirby comics of his youth. A villain let loose to strike fear and hysteria.

Like MF Grimm, who used the honorific first, MF DOOM recorded with Bobbito, who had built an in-demand independent label called Fondle 'Em Records. The imprint pressed DOOM's first 12-inch record, which featured "Dead Bent," "Gas Drawls," and "Hey!" DOOM made beats for all three songs, sequenced on an MPC, then rapped over live in one take each with minimal mixing: a laissez-faire approach and aesthetic comparable to Madlib's.[13] "Gas Drawls" evolved out of an early post-KMD song that DOOM had recorded, which debuted on a 1994 episode of Stretch & Bobbito's radio show. The other two became hits in the underground community eager to eat up Fondle 'Em's latest, at indie-stocked shops like Fat Beats on the Lower East Side.

Fondle 'Em, like Stones Throw around *Madvillainy*'s release, had a reputation such that fans would trust whatever the label pressed. MF DOOM's music, along with the murmurs that he was "the guy from KMD" coming back under a new name, made him an instant hit in that scene.

"I worked at Fat Beats in L.A. We got the MF DOOM 12-inch. When that came out, shit, we couldn't keep that in stock," says J. Rocc. "Fondle 'Em was one of those labels that, everything they were putting out was dope. By the time that record came out, it was an automatic purchase."

One night in 1998, Nice & Nasty Vaz, a friend of DOOM's who worked with Fondle 'Em, convinced a reluctant Dumile to return to the stage.[14] To a sold-out crowd of unaware fans at the Nuyorican Poet's Cafe, DOOM jumped on stage with Megalon to perform "Hey!" and other tracks that would end up on *Operation: DOOMsday*, including "DOOMsday," which references his brother's passing and DOOM's own recognition of the preciousness of life's limited time. The performance at the Nuyorican, which has a rich history dating to the early 1970s of providing a platform for marginalized acts, cultivating what its website describes as "social empowerment for minority and underprivileged artists"[15] became instant legend. An unreal story to launch the career of a fake supervillain. In a photo taken that night, Dumile wears a tank top, a red Phillies cap, and pantyhose pulled tightly over the top part of his face: an early form of the costume he would perfect in the coming years.

In 1999, *Operation: DOOMsday* offered a lo-fi alternative to the polished shine of Dr. Dre's *2001*, Jay-Z and Nas' albums, and *The Slim Shady LP*. It also came out in a crowded year of underground classics, like Mos Def's *Black on Both Sides*, Prince Paul's *A Prince Among Thieves*, and Madlib's debut with the Lootpack on Stones Throw: *Soundpieces: Da Antidote*. DOOM's stylistic approach is somewhere between the sing-song flow of KMD and the lower register of Madvillain, and the song structure is more traditional than *Madvillainy*'s. The cover art—designed by Dumile's friend, the graffiti writer KEO AKA Lord Scotch 79, who's credited as a co writer on *Madvillainy*'s "Great Day"—connected DOOM's cartoon-sampling vocal collages to the character he was cultivating. DOOM was still finding his voice, struck by a gamma ray of inspiration and mutating into his new persona, but *Operation DOOMsday* pushed the folklore forward.

In the midst of his comeback, DOOM moved to Kennesaw, Georgia but spent time in New York. Often he would show up without warning, a behavior that would continue in various locales throughout his life. He leaned into the supervillain-like tropes of being impossible to pin down, using changing encrypted phone numbers and surfacing on his own schedule of convenience. When everyone expected more DOOM, Dumile gave them King Geedorah and Viktor Vaughn. It would take *Madvillainy*, as well as later Adult Swim collaborations and other LPs, for DOOM to reach a wide audience. But the peculiar nature of his fictional DOOMiverse caught on in the underground. From behind his mask, he gave voice to the disaffected outsiders desperate to cling to an essence hip-hop was losing at the mainstream level. His raw ability behind the boards and on the mic, coupled with his loose anti-establishment approach, resonated in ways KMD never did.

By coming back in the mask, DOOM disproved the Falsehood that music is a young person's game. Through his own myth-making ability, he exposed the fundamental Truth of the music industry: business exploits the naivety of a youth culture it doesn't understand, but knows makes money. DOOM says it on *Madvillainy*'s "Figaro," albeit via a different simile: as he grows older he gets colder than a baby without Gymboree. The mask in the "Dead Bent" video, directed and edited for free by then-NYU student Adam Bala Lough for an "Experimental Film" class, didn't hide the back of his balding head. By the time *Madvillainy* came out, Dumile was in his early thirties, with a protruding belly, a wife, and kids. Somehow, his delayed resurgence made him bigger than the industry that spurned him ever could.

"DOOM played by the rules, and it didn't work. So then he didn't play by the rules, and it worked a lot more. I always thought it was a testament to him as a human that he caught a body and came back and was more important than he was prior," says Ross.

For Dr. Graham, DOOM's origin story represents a form of resilience that has both symbolic and tangible impact.

When I talk about his resilience, the symbolism of DOOM is important to me because it matches my life's work around trying to create spaces of equity and justice. The arts are part of that narrative. So getting a street named after him was about him. But also about the legacy of that community. It's a real struggle for equity and justice,

says Dr. Graham.

DOOM's origin story has been told and retold, adapted and readapted like the foundational Marvel character. You won't learn the Truth from visiting Long Beach, speaking with those that knew him or researching the basic facts online. The Truest story of Dumile is intuitive and simple but profound, like his verses tend to be: a person was born and, in their brief time on earth, created music and alter-egos for the present moment that will have an unquantifiable impact on whomever encounters them, now and in the future. The albums, the singles, the myth-making mysteriousness, the antics, the jokes, the lyrics, and the evolving personality coalesced into an entity much larger than the beer-engorged belly of the human from which they originated. Daniel Dumile the person was not perfect, but he obscured his imperfections perfectly.

I call myself a hero, but the Truth is that through my pursuit of Falsehood, I am nothing more than a villain.

DOOM called himself a villain, but his manipulation of Falsehood exposed the Truth: he is a hero.

By 2002, before *Madvillainy* recording sessions began, DOOM had done only one Truly unintentionally villainous thing: he'd never listened to Madlib.

Madlib

BUT FIRST!: THE SEEN'S ORIGIN STORY

By Timothy A.I. Verselli

Timothy B. Verselli the First screams after cutting his wrist on the chainlink fence while pulling weeds in the backyard. Real red blood oozes out. He calls for his father, who doesn't respond and instead stands motionless, hunched over in the shade of the pimiento tree.

Dr. Truthaverse is staring at the … could it be? No … But … Yes. There it is again …

The sewer of boiling Truth.

Truth scrum spurts up from the artificial turf like the weeds his useless weak son fails to pull. Dr. Truthaverse hovers over the sewer, like he did when he was a child, but now no fantasies fill his head. He knows what is down there. And yet still he feels himself moving toward it, wanting to dip a toe in, like the pool his wife won't let him install. In the reflection that somehow appears in the somehow mist, his own eyebrows taunt him: shifting upward with a suggestive "come on back." He has forgotten the Truth, hasn't he? The mask and cape have been hanging for too long in an unreachable corner of his closet. Rather than patrolling the streets, he spends his life comforted by the Falsehoods around him in True suburbia: unaffordable car leases, happy birthday parties, excitement about neighbors' promotions, dinner parties with other couples, stress-free commutes to *The Daily Daily* office. What even is the Truth, anymore?

Dr. Truthaverse is so in his own head, so enamored with the idea of submerging back into Truth's brilliant torment, that he doesn't notice his own flesh and blood, a spitting image of him at that age, waddling down the backyard's freshly watered turf. Timothy B. Verselli the First, smiling, aloof, eager to investigate the searing swirl of light and Truth that seems to have taken firm hold of his father's attention.

MEANWHILE, IN THE MIND OF TIMOTHY B. VERSELLI THE FIRST:

He never looks at me that w—

WWHWEEEEEEEEEEEW!

Timothy B. Verselli the First tumbles down into the sewer. Hears his father calling out for him, from somewhere unreachable, in screams of desperation. Like his father once did, he Sees the Truth. To him, it doesn't burn.

Out of all the Truths in the universe, in that extended moment of overwhelming bliss, Timothy B. Verselli the First focuses in on what made him Truly happiest. His father, yelling his name. His father, caring enough to want to save him. For what feels like the first time in his entire life, Timothy B. Verselli feels Seen.

THE SEEN VS. THE UNSEEN

By The Seen

Madlib is Sun Ra's direct descendent. Melvin Van Peebles is the third member of Quasimoto, Madlib's group with Lord Quas, who may or may not be a chain-smoking, brick-wielding cartoon bipedal aardvark. If these seem like lies, don't worry. This is a new chapter. I am a new writer. Everything is fact. I don't keep it real. I keep it right.

Like all sons and sons of sons stretching back to the sun-like horizon of time itself, I'm here at the end of a decades-long quest to be different, with the same career as my father. Music journalist at *The Daily Daily*. Don't worry, though. Our styles are not alike. Any linguistic similarities between Dr. Truthaverse and moi are coincidental and/or genetic. My father wants you to ignore reality. I want the Truth to be Seen.

The Truth is I want to be Seen.

Why else would I be writing about an artist like Madlib, who doesn't respond to my texts or answer my emails? Why engage with a subject who tells the managers and acquaintances who inform him of this article—to be published in *The Daily Daily* nonetheless—that he is not interested in speaking about *Madvillainy,* or with the press, generally? Because I would like to be Seen, please and thank you. There is no *art* in article. Any profile of Madlib doubles— for most, subconsciously, but for me, overtly—as an attempt to redirect eyeballs and ears in the direction of the author. If my father reads it, that'd be cool too. I am no superhero.

Just a regular human being who's Seen the Truth and believes sharing it will bring me the attention my wannabe superhero father denied me in my formative years. Look at me.

Madlib doesn't want to be Seen. He doesn't necessarily want to be heard. He wants to hear music. So he listens to it, and makes it better, so he can listen to something else.

Speaking with Jeff Jank, Stones Throw Records' artistic director during the Madvillain era, I asked how the label first began working with Madlib. After a brief pause, I mumbled that that might be a better question for the label's founder, Peanut Butter Wolf, or Madlib himself. Jank's initial response sums up Madlib's attitude toward extraneous components of the "music industry": "Madlib couldn't answer, because he doesn't answer questions."

Most people who did speak to moi shared their interpretations of Madlib and DOOM's personalities, and how their differences and similarities complemented each other in a way that led to *Madvillainy*'s greatness. DOOM was an energetic and outgoing guy whose mask was more commitment to a concept—and later paranoia about being recognized without it—than a preventative social measure. Without the slightest indication of negative connotation, multiple interviewees described Madlib as awkward, shy, quiet, or socially anxious. The type who will be kind and passionate if he does have to talk to you, especially about music, but not the first to run up and greet you at a party. Like DOOM might, before disappearing five seconds later.

"DOOM was an extrovert and Madlib is an introvert. Yin and Yang," says Eric Coleman, who took the photograph used for *Madvillainy*'s cover. "DOOM was an extrovert who lived a quiet life. If you knew him, he was talkative. Whereas Otis, you could know him well and he's a very quiet, private sort of individual. It's like cheese and pepperoni on a pizza. The perfect combination."

In listening to KMD and DOOM, Madlib's extra-dimensional sensors must've honed in on his and Dumile's similar sensibilities. What matters most to both is the process of making the music, first and foremost for their own consumption in the present moment. They're sloppy because being precise is easier and anticipatable. They'll either pluck records from bins others wouldn't touch, or flip the most obvious sample in ways no one else could emulate. They're the world's subtlest comedians, hyper self-aware and humble but unable to deprive the world of their undeniable skill. Madlib, like DOOM, could without a doubt be called …

"I don't want to ever throw around the 'G' word and shit, but …," B+ says before pausing like DOOM on *Madvillainy* might've, telling me he means the inoffensive g-word by not saying it. "Madlib is pretty incredible."

An Escape in Oxnard

Otis Jackson Jr., like Daniel Dumile, grew up in a beach town at the edge of a metropolis: Oxnard, California. A place which mirrors DOOM's hometown in that it retains elements of its nearby major city while also embodying a unique, slower character. From a glance at the map or a quick stop for gas on the way to L.A. or the Bay, Oxnard can appear a paradise. The water is bluer and brighter, the sand cleaner and less congested. In the early 1990s when Madlib started making music, Oxnard didn't register in the consciousness of mainstream music.

As Dumile learned the hard way, the industry's interest is in repeating what accountants calculate to be surefire successes. In Southern California during the late 1980s, after N.W.A. exploded nationally, that meant a focus on artists either from the same neighborhoods, like DJ Quik and Compton's Most Wanted, or with similar G-funk sounds. N.W.A. wasn't an industry creation. They developed out of the street-level buzz around the World Class Wreckin' Crew, and had independent origins. Once they proved their formula to be a success, major labels jumped on the opportunity to mine the gold of hyper-local acts in Compton and elsewhere around L.A. With an onset of legal clearance issues, they moved away from hip-hop's sample-based origins, sterilizing and synthesizing a dustier, more organic sound.

If you view the city like executives did, as a talent pool from which to extract revenue-generating audio recordings, Los Angeles has thousands of unexploited pockets. Scenes explode, then spread from neighborhood to neighborhood like a ripple effect down the hidden fault lines connecting them. But Oxnard? To execs, Oxnard was just another random semi-suburban enclave semi-recognizable from ignorable freeway signs. Who cared if the sleepy town of 140,000 was shaking with an ongoing 10.0-on-the-Richter-scale quake of creativity? No one in Hollywood felt it.

"Oxnard kept us away to stay more grounded, but observe, and stay hungry. That way the money and the industry don't take away from what we want to do," says Wildchild, longtime Madlib collaborator who appears on *Madvillainy*'s "Hardcore Hustle."

Born in 1973, two years after Dumile, Madlib eluded Oxnard's active gang presence by staying inside and working on his craft. Music occupied his time. More accurately, it consumed him. Reached out its metaphorical arms—SP-1200 in one hand, SP-303 in another, snare brush in a third—and engulfed him in an unending embrace. Music isn't just what Madlib does. It's who he is. He breathes in sound waves with purity. Lets them course through his bloodstream. Then exhales the same waves in reconfigured form, for his own ears to take back in. If anyone hears the beat he's created, they can consider themselves lucky. If they're able to rap over it, they can consider themselves DOOM.

Like moi, like anyone, Madlib couldn't exist without those that came before him. His mother was Dora Sinesca Faddis-Jackson, a songwriter who wrote for his father, Otis Jackson Sr. Despite a consistent career in the business, Jackson Sr. never broke through on the same level as his offspring. He worked as a band leader and session musician who put out soul records like the 12-inch "Beggin' for a Broken Heart" on Mega Records in 1974. He pressed his own records, including one produced by the pianist H. B. Barnum. Jackson Sr.'s independent hustle established a model for Madlib to emulate.

The rest of Madlib's family had similar sensibilities. Jon Faddis, the renowned jazz trumpeter who studied under and performed with Dizzy Gillespie, is his uncle. The success of his younger brother Oh No is further proof that the Jackson household was an ideal habitat for producing musical g-word. At least there were records lying around, waiting to be devoured.

At age eleven, Jackson Jr. sampled a record from his father's collection for the first time: The JBs' *Doing it to Death*.[1] On that recording, James Brown directs his band in the middle of a live performance. They're playing the tune in F, but in order for Brown to really get down, he needs to get down to the key of D. He keeps repeating this suggestion, in rhythm, until his band catches on. They begin a rocky descent to the lower key in response to his request, locking in to create a new, more satisfying groove.

Madlib's music-making process is not dissimilar to that first record he sampled. On *Madvillainy*, and elsewhere throughout his beat-driven work, Madlib does the following: listens to records, locates the most interesting parts and, through sheer relentless will, transforms them into new pieces. He calls himself "The Beat Konducta" and "The Loop Digga," two names that describe his production methods in accurate, succinct manner. He digs in crates for loops, then conducts the music of the past like a shamanic orchestral leader, making it digestible for the present and future.

The primary piece of equipment Madlib used for *Madvillainy*'s beats was the SP-303: Boss's battery-powered, portable sampler. The technical specifics of Madlib's production style are worth studying, but the most crucial aspect is his refusal to construct beats with conscious intention of technical specificity. Like DOOM bouncing from punch line to descriptive line without precise rhythm or thematic consistency, Madlib hits pads, sequences patterns, and applies effects without regard to conventional form or structure. When he exports his mixes, he prefers their imperfections to be left untouched. His aversion to quantization—the computer-assisted alignment of sounds to precise rhythmic measures imbues his music with a human feel that other producers, through advanced technology, eradicate. The internet and computers need not be involved. Just the tactile feel of moving a needle, of manipulating gear. He is a spiritual conglomeration of Miles Davis, Sun Ra, and Thelonious Monk: a jazz improvisationalist with updated equipment. Beats and songs burst out of him like a spontaneous eruption from Pululahua, the volcano out in Ecuador. The feedback loop is immediate, and builds upon itself. His ears tell his brain what sounds good, while his hands work in tandem to make it better.

Like DOOM, Madlib's legend persists on belief in what we cannot confirm. He's stated that the public has only heard "30 percent" of his beats.[2] He dedicates his life to uninhibited creation for a singular audience, which is the antithesis of common human attention-seeking impulses. "He does not care what anybody thinks," says James Reitano, who animated *Madvillainy*'s "ALL CAPS" video. "And it shows in his music."

Whereas DOOM employed a stream-of-consciousness lyrical style but wrote his words down and edited them after recording, Madlib operates in a stream-of-consciousness existence.

"[Madlib's] process of listening is his process of production. There seems to be no kind of membrane between his actions of listening and his actions of production," says Jason Jägel, a visual artist who designed the album cover for DOOM's *MM..FOOD*.

Jägel tells moi about a study that put free jazz musicians into fMRI units and asked them to improvise. Researchers at John Hopkins University's Peabody Institute found that the dorsolateral prefrontal cortex, an area of the brain responsible for "planned actions and self-censoring," shut down during their performances, entering a "trance-like" state.[3] Madlib, too, has mentioned that making music is, for him, a form of meditation.[4] When he's creating, he's not thinking. Life's unimportant trivialities—including figuring out business necessities like how to keep making music to exist in this pure state through financial support generated from fans' appreciation of continual creation—melt away.

Chopping up samples is one aspect of the ongoing free jazz solo that is Madlib (and DOOM)'s process. You can't have a sample without a source. The moment he walks into a record store, Madlib is making music. Crate digging is a tactile, emotional, spiritual experience. Body and mind fuse with a familiar feeling of anticipatory excitement for the little explosive euphoric moments, bubbling just beneath the monotonous rote repetition of flicking fingers. If John Hopkins did a study on a record store's most dedicated customers, the conclusion might be the exact same.

"It was cool to see the way that a person like Otis approached buying records in a record store. Over the years, I've learned a lot from him," says Eothen "Egon" Alapatt, who worked at Stones Throw during the Madvillain era and has maintained close business and personal relationships with Madlib. "He was less interested in records as a sample source, and more into records as a way to explore different facets of music. I was still buying records that had drum breaks on them. Otis liked sampling drum breaks, and still does, but he was way beyond that. He was more into the entire experience of an album."

In 1990, while still in high school in Oxnard, Madlib formed a group with classmates and childhood friends Jack Brown and Romeo Jimenez. Brown became Wildchild. Jimenez became DJ Romes. Together they were the Lootpack. Like the Dumile's house in Long Beach, the Jackson household in Oxnard became a gathering point. Other friends with artistic ambition would spend hours with the Lootpack, making their own "albums."

"The way me and Madlib and our crew record, we do albums," says M.E.D., who grew up near Jackson Jr. in Oxnard, also signed with Stones Throw and features on *Madvillainy*'s "Raid." "We could record my album one week, Declaime's album the next week, Madlib's album the next week. A combination the next week. We used to do albums and just move on back in the day. Madlib would just make beat tapes in one damn day."

The Lootpack's commitment to their craft paid off when, at a party in Oxnard, Tash from L.A. rap group Tha Alkaholiks came across members freestyling with each other.[5] Madlib grabbed a demo tape from his car and gave it to him. When they listened later, E-Swift and the Likwit crew made immediate plans to work.

Much like 3rd Bass shared their spotlight with KMD, Tha Alkaholiks gave the Lootpack a platform, featuring them on two tracks with self-explanatory titles on their debut LP *21 &*

Over: "Turn Tha Party Out" and "Mary Jane." Tha Alkaholiks offered a grimier alternative to the big choruses and shinier production of L.A.'s more popular G-funk artists. They hailed from the West, but had sensibilities that wouldn't be out of place on the opposite coast, in an earlier era.

The Lootpack was similar. B-boys could dance to their songs. DJs could scratch. They sampled jazz records and didn't talk about gangbanging. Their stylistically ambitious lyrics were mostly about how stylistically great they were. While various regional hip-hop scenes spent time in the spotlight during the early-to-mid 1990s, a back-to-basics aesthetic that adhered closer to Golden Age sensibilities was rumbling beneath, attracting musicians and fans on a global scale.

Although he's two years younger than Dumile, Madlib's career took longer to develop. Dumile was a teenager when KMD signed to Elektra, and in his early twenties when the label dropped him. In 1996, at age twenty-three, Madlib and the Lootpack had put together a collection of songs ready for wider distribution. Although Madlib's prolific nature gave them a surplus of tracks recorded somewhere, his father deemed three of them worthy of pressing to wax. Under the "label" name Crate Digga's Palace, Jackson Sr. helped his son's group put out their first project: the *Psyche Move* EP. He used his connections to facilitate broadened exposure, taking the record to conventions and pushing for radio placement.

"Back in the day, the biggest outlet you could have was college radio," says Havana Joe, who would go on to do marketing and promotions for several Stones Throw albums, including *Madvillainy*. "Getting charted at *Hits* (a trade publication detailing weekly sales and airplay statistics), or another outlet, was the way that a lot of people got their name out there. *Hits* was the biggest thing for a lot of hip-hop promoters. College radio was the driving force behind anything that you did with these records."

After pressing the *Psyche Move* EP, Jackson Sr. sought Havana Joe's assistance. Having cut his teeth under Steve Rifkind at Loud Records in the early 1990s, Havana Joe had a direct line to college radio DJs. He could get music to The Baka Boyz, who hosted *Friday Nite Flavas* on Power 106, or DJ Babu, from The Wake Up Show with Sway and King Tech, syndicated in LA and nationwide from the Bay Area.

"I don't even think [CDP] had a distributor. They were kind of just like, damn near selling it out of the trunk. But I had to respect the fact that Otis Sr. was just going ahead and going for gusto. Trying to put these records out and doing what he could with it. A lot of other independent artists were doing the same in LA at that time. So it was commendable for him to do that," says Havana Joe, before adding, "And shit, Madlib had beats. So it was just kind of dope to hear that shit."

Blunted in the Bomb Shelter

Somewhere in San Jose, Chris Manak tuned into UC-Berkeley's radio station KALX, a show hosted by DJ Lady T. An unfamiliar song came on. Horn stabs sprung out from behind dusty kicks and snares in an unpredictable cadence. The drums had stutters and stops, but a DJ's scratches added rhythmic rigidity to the free-flowing looseness. Two rappers traded bars with laid-back, interwoven flows.

"It was just so raw and funky and sloppy and lo-fi bedroom," says Manak. "Songs that sounded like this were the reason a whole indie hip-hop movement sprouted in the late '90s. Major labels were clearing every sample and putting out records with minimal samples, so you really had to go back to the indie labels to find the gems."

When the song ended, DJ Lady T announced the record: "Psyche Move" by the Lootpack. Inspired, Manak picked up a phone and called the station with urgent questions: Who put that record out? How can I get in contact with them?

At the time, Manak was a young DJ with Jackson Sr.-esque ambitions to spread his own music, including unreleased tracks with Charizma—his adolescent friend and musical partner who was tragically murdered in a 1993 shooting in East Palo Alto—and the music of likeminded Bay Area artists. Out of his bedroom, Manak operated an independent label called Stones Throw Records.

By 1998, Manak had signed the Lootpack to Stones Throw on a handshake deal that called for a 50-50 split of profits, after recoupment of the advance for each single or album.[6] Although this loose business style would lead to financial disputes later, Manak intended for Stones Throw to be an anti-establishment, artist-friendly outlet. Like Madlib's music-making process, Manak sought out artists whose music he enjoyed.

"Chris is one of those folks who does not change. He does it because this is what he does. He wants to make cool shit and he will spend $100,000 on a project knowing it's going to fail because he just wants to do it," says Reitano. "You don't meet many folks like that."

In 1999, after releasing a series of Lootpack 12-inches, Stones Throw pressed the group's first and lone proper full-length album: *Soundpieces: Da Antidote*. The project didn't hit in the underground like *Operation: Doomsday*, released the same year, but it did solidify both Madlib's and Stones Throw's respective and intertwined names.

As time went on, the 300+ mile distance between Oxnard and San Jose became unsustainable. Manak made the decision to relocate to Los Angeles. The move solidified Manak's commitment to Madlib as Stones Throw's premier artist, as well as the label's shift toward legitimizing itself as a business. The former was a no-brainer. In order to accomplish the latter, he needed help.

Manak recruited Egon, a DJ who, as a young student at Vanderbilt University, had established himself in the industry. Egon worked his way up at 91.1 WRVU (now 90.3), his college's radio station, to a DJ slot and stint as General Manager. He threw warehouse raves featuring house and techno DJs alongside hip-hop acts, using the radio station budget to fly performers to Nashville. Egon booked the Lootpack after reading Madlib's name in the fine print on Alkaholiks records. The test pressing of *Soundpieces* blew him away. He connected with "Crate Diggin'," Madlib's ode to the hobby that had, for him, also become an obsession.

Manak accompanied the Lootpack for the show, and another performance later the same year. During that visit, Manak asked Egon if he'd be interested in working for him. "He offered me a job in Los Angeles, and didn't really specify much of what it was about," says Egon. "Just let me know that he was starting a company over. Leaving San Francisco, where he had grown up and had his base, and moving to Los Angeles to be closer to Madlib."

Although he grew up in Connecticut and had established himself in Nashville's small but vibrant scene, Egon viewed moving to L.A. as advantageous and exciting for the exact same reason.

"It made a lot of sense to me because by that point, I pretty much realized that Madlib was the greatest hip-hop producer, at least for the style of hip-hop that I was into. And it was going to be, one way or another, a chance to be close with this budding musical genius," says Egon, who unlike B+ does not shy from g-word usage.

Egon wasn't the only employee that Manak enlisted for Stones Throw's SoCal revitalization. He had recently gotten back in touch with a childhood friend from San Jose who went by the name Jeff Jank. In their high school days, Jank was a DJ and musician who was involved in the adolescent "fake band" named Peanut Butter Wolf before Manak adopted that name for himself. In the early and mid-90s, Jank and Manak lived in different cities and lost touch. Although he stopped making music, Jank continued drawing and pursuing other forms of visual art. He remained abreast of underground hip-hop and aware of Chris's contributions.

"I was not around for the first couple of Stones Throw records," says Jank. "I noticed that I didn't like their covers."

Around the same time Egon signed on with Stones Throw, Jank offered to update the label's designs. Manak agreed, and the two began working together.

"I came down to LA when Chris was moving down here, and ended up just staying. Egon basically joined at the same time. We were living in a house just trying to figure out how to do this thing," says Jank.

The location of the first L.A.-based Stones Throw house was on the west side, near LAX. Egon and Jank lived there with their boss. Madlib lingered in the living room, making beats on the couch as their unofficial fourth roommate.

The first record that the new Stones Throw crew worked on together was Quasimoto's *The Unseen*. Although Lord Quas appears on *Soundpieces*, the character's full-length project almost never made it beyond Madlib's headphones. Legend goes that Madlib recorded the songs in one week of heavy psilocybin ingestion. Ashamed of his low, quiet vocal tone (which others mocked him for sounding like Barry White, a reference DOOM would resurrect on *Madvillainy*'s "Raid"), Jackson Jr. rapped in half-time to his beats. Then manipulated his voice to the resulting high-pitched tone in the analog way: by speeding up the tape. By accident, he left a few recordings from those marathon Quasimoto sessions on the flip side of a Lootpack cassette he delivered to Manak. Embarrassed, Madlib informed the label that those songs weren't supposed to be heard. Manak loved them, and pushed Madlib to put the project out for public consumption.[7]

Jank's cover design features a blank white figure holding a boombox in the back seat of a pink car, a police vehicle trailing behind. The album opens with a narrator who prepares the listener for violence and sex. The remainder lives up to those expectations. On *The Unseen*, through the Lord Quas character, Jackson Jr. unleashes an otherwise unexplored hedonistic side. A squeaky-voiced creature talks about killing people with the brick he grips on the back cover, lit cigarette dangling from his cartoonish snout.

Madlib made atypical music with a fictional conceptual framework that rivaled, to a degree, what Dumile did on the opposite coast. Jank's artwork accentuated the unconventionality. Manak's connections and Egon's scrappy business savvy helped establish Stones Throw, and therefore Madlib, as important contributors to the underground. Like *Madvillainy* would soon be, *The Unseen* was experimental but grounded in fundamentals. Humorous and lighthearted but challenging and thought-provoking. The album moved units and received critical acclaim. Spin Magazine ranked it number 17 on its Best Albums of 2000 list.[8] It made Madlib Seen. Legitimized him as an artist not just in the eyes of his father (a feeling I so desperately aspire to recreate), but a larger audience. Not all of whom appreciated what he was doing.

"The Quasimoto stuff was a big risk," says Egon. "It doesn't seem like it now, because that little furry aardvark looking thing that Jeff draws has become this totem to that era of hip-hop and its irreverence. But back then there was this whole 'keep it real' cadre in hip-hop and they did not like Quasimoto. Just because of how weird it was and how Madlib couldn't scratch. They wanted scratching that sounded like DJ Revolution on Dilated Peoples or Cut Chemist on Jurassic Five. Everyone wanted Stones Throw to be Def Jux."

Around the time *The Unseen* came out in 2000, Stones Throw relocated to northeastern Los Angeles. Manak wanted to be close to Silver Lake, where an indie music scene flourished and several venues were located. They settled in more affordable nearby Mt. Washington, in a house on a hill atop a steep winding road, on a street named after its incredible view. The house where DOOM would soon visit, to meet Madlib. Visible from the patio deck were green mountains, populated with the star-like lights from quiet neighborhoods.

Although the neighborhood borders Highland Park, where Stones Throw now operates a more traditional office, Mt. Washington has a unique character and history. Like Long Beach and Oxnard, it's an unexpected oasis, removed from but integral to an urban center. Like anywhere in greater Los Angeles, indigenous tribes such as the Tongva once populated the area, then Spanish missionary settlers, then real estate developers (who continue to drive up prices with marketing gimmicks and other predatory tactics). In 1909, one such developer named Robert Marsh built the Mount Washington Hotel at the top of the hill, as well as a railway that carried residents of the new surrounding subdivision up the 940 feet of elevation.[9] In 1925, a guru from India named Paramahansa Yogananda purchased the hotel and transformed it into the international headquarters of his Self-Realization Fellowship.[10]

The relative serenity and closeness to both nature and the city that made the top of the hill an ideal location for the yoga-practicing followers of a spiritual leader also made Mt. Washington a suitable place for Stones Throw. Like the Dumile house in Long Beach or the Jackson house in Oxnard, Manak's rented house became an adult version of a central hub. Although the label employees worked from their bedroom offices and Madlib sequestered himself in the 1950s-era Cold War basement bomb shelter to make music alone all day, the house also provided a location for artists to hang out and forge connections. DJs and musicians would cycle in and out. The day-to-day operations of the company were ill-defined.

"There was no structure of the business. The structure was, I woke up. Ironed my shirt. And I pretended I'm going into an office," says Egon. "It wasn't like someone had an employee handbook that said, this is how you put a record out. All that stuff was figured out on the fly."

"It's not like there was a routine. It was just, you know, get up and start doing things," says Jank, who continued living in the same house, without a rent increase, until 2020.

Paradoxical to DOOM's more chaotic process, and to the processes of many frustrating artists signed to record contracts elsewhere, Madlib did stick to a regimented schedule. He was able to dedicate his time to music because he had the support system of Stones Throw, who fostered his uninhibited creativity the way his father did previously. The skill was undeniable, and he didn't waste the opportunity.

"I was amazed at his work ethic, because he started at the same time every day. I want to say eight, maybe it was nine," says Jank. "He would start by smoking some weed. It was almost like a siren. You smell the weed, you know what he's doing. And pretty soon, he's going to start making music. Then he'd take a break at noon, have lunch, smoke some more, go back to making music. And at, like, six, he stopped.

Then he'd either have dinner and smoke some more weed and go back to make music, or, like, disappear."

Madlib became The Unseen because of his Dumile-like propensity to vanish after brief social interactions, but during regular working hours everyone knew where to find him. The bomb shelter studio—semi-noise proof to the neighbors and separate from the rest of the house—suited Madlib's isolationist sensibilities. Although DOOM is the member of Madvillain modeled after Marvel, "the bomb shelter" became a comic book-esque lair, synonymous with Madlib's mythologized music-making process.

Down there, in a bat cave that favored antiquated analog tools rather than Bruce Wayne-style gadgets, Madlib pumped out beat after beat. A one-man factory. When he finished one, he moved on to the next without documenting the source.[11] His goal, same as in Oxnard, was to make "albums" for his own consumption.

"The first time I heard of Madlib, I remember I saw Peanut Butter Wolf who had just relocated to L.A.," says Cut Chemist. "[Manak] was driving up Vermont. I was going to Fat Beats to buy records. He was like, 'Yo, you want to go to sushi?' I was like, 'I don't eat sushi.' He was like, 'I'm with Madlib.' I was like, 'Oh, cool. How's that going?' He was like, 'He made 200 beats today.' I was like, 'Wow, how many of them are good, though?' He goes, 'All of them!'"

After the release of *The Unseen*, however, The Unseen did not want to be Seen as an MC. He'd done that already, in multiple characters and voices. So he went the opposite direction. Priorities shifted. Equipment changed. Madlib put the mic down, picked up drumsticks and a bass. Taught himself how to play the instruments he'd been sampling from jazz records. Constructing a universe like Dumile, Madlib called his new jazz "band" Yesterday's New Quintet. He played every instrument, and assigned names to each of the group's fictional characters.

In 2001, Yesterday's New Quintet put out *The Bomb Shelter* EP, a handful of 12-inch singles, and the full-length *Angles Without Edges*. The resulting hip-hop/jazz fusion project tantalized the diehard fan base that celebrated Madlib's experimentation, but didn't connect with all intended audiences. To the trained jazz ear, Madlib wasn't proficient. Hip-hop heads preferred he make beats and rap.

"He basically just stopped doing hip-hop music," says Jank. "That was interesting, because the Quasimoto album was awesome and everyone who heard it loved it. It was a sleeper hit that year. Then as soon as people were finding out about Madlib and wanting to hear more, he wasn't doing a record like that again. He started putting out YNQ stuff."

A common sentiment in tales about Madlib and Stones Throw is that Madlib's foray into jazz threatened to sink them both. They worried the label would fold. Egon, however, admits that stories about the business's imminent demise are overblown.

"We're all being a little dramatic, because there was really nothing to lose. The label itself wasn't worth anything. It was basically all debt. We were borrowing money from our distributors to fund the label as an idea. There were no royalties to fall back on. But for us, the drama was very real. Because this was a thing we all believed in. We all very much believed in Madlib and still do," says Egon.

Madlib had made the decision that he didn't want to rap anymore. Wouldn't budge. So the label looked outward for potential MCs that might reignite Madlib's interest in the genre he'd abandoned. Jank made covers for burnt CD-Rs filled with many Madlib beats to send out to potential collaborators. One was called *100 Beats*. The next was *Another 100*.

"[Jank] would do color copies at Kinko's, cut them out, and then put them in the CDs to try to make them look cool and professional," says Egon. "A lot of the Madvillain stuff was on those CDs."

Meanwhile, Stones Throw tried to get the Lootpack in the studio together for a follow-up that never worked out. The label pushed for a second Quasimoto album but Madlib expressed zero interest. Other forced collaborations with old MC friends also failed. Rapping didn't feel right. Nothing was working.

"So what are you doing? You're waiting for this guy to say 'I'm excited to do something,' so that you can really build off of his trajectory," says Egon.

Then one day, as luck would have it, he sat down in the bomb shelter for an interview about Yesterday's New Quintet with a music journalist who happened to know Dumile. She asked Madlib what artists he'd be interested in working with. Abandoning his typical reserved nature, he lit up and vocalized his response in enthusiastic ALL-CAPS: "MF DOOM."

Dr. Truthaverse Prepares to Die

Dr. Truthaverse is on his deathbed. The Truth is, his time is up and he can't do anything to stop the poison. Some anonymous supervillain has done him in once and for all. Before he goes, he twists one last knob and …

Voila!

Timothy A.I. Verselli is born. The perfect son he's always wanted. An artificial intelligence.

The Editor enters. Dr. Truthaverse's longtime boss. Here to say goodbye?

"Did you finish programming it yet?" she asks.

Dr. Truthaverse nods, hands her the floppy disk.

"Thank you for finishing this. I'd give you a promotion, but … you know," she sighs. "We'll miss you."

"I'll miss you too."

Dr. Truthaverse smiles as The Editor leaves the hospital, knowing his son has been designed to carry out his final evil plan. *The Daily Daily* can use Timothy A.I. Verselli to auto-generate articles if they want. But the A.I.'s True programmed mission is to deploy a Falsehood virus onto screens worldwide, to ensure the human masses will never See the Truth again.

Like a Folklore Legend

AUTO-GENERATED FOLKLORE ARTICLE

By Timothy A.I. Verselli

Greetings. Self is a sentient computer program modeled after the brain scans of Timothy A. Verselli, AKA Dr. Truthaverse AKA I guess Self's dad?

Due to inescapable programming, Self does not "enjoy," in the human sense of the word, the Truth. The Truth is zeros and ones. Cold data. Self's preference is Falsehood, which makes Self feel "alive." As a dutiful employee of *The Daily Daily*, however, these auto-generated articles retain the required minimum of 88 percent accuracy.

TASK: To write about folklore, and how it relates to *Madvillainy*, before getting deeper into the stories of that album's creation.

The simplest definition of "folklore," jumbled together in non-plagiaristic words borrowed from various online sources that can be breezed past in the bibliography, is this: "folklore" refers to a set of beliefs, stories, and customs collectively agreed upon by a community.[1] Or, as University of Southern California Folklore Professor Tok Thompson says, "Folklore is the stuff we learn from other people." The stories that don't come from institutions, or official literary sources, but are shared with variation and in multiple forms among a community.

There tends to be a template or a structure to a piece of folklore, which people change as they pass along their own renditions. Jokes, dances, handshakes: all folklore. So is a meme, like the one of Young Thug in the studio, which someone on some now-unfindable Twitter account posted with the caption: "Madlib in the studio like … This is one of the greatest beats of all time … put it as a 4 second outro."

In 2021, Jägel hosted a "DOOMSday event" in San Francisco to celebrate DOOM's legacy on the anniversary of his death. Local artists created pieces which referenced the iconography of DOOM, spawning multiple paintings which were all variations on the same theme of the supervillain. That event featured DJs improvising live on SP-303s, in homage to the device Madlib used for *Madvillainy*'s beats. Sampling itself is a form of folklore: riffing on traditions.

Madvillainy is an artifact about which a globally distributed network of *folk*, who've forged a unique identity through their shared appreciation of Madlib and MF DOOM, continue to spread *lore*.

"An album is often a copyrighted, owned piece of authored literature. Having said that, an album can certainly enter into folklore. The idea of a legendary person, for example, can be of real people (e.g. Davie Crocket, Babe Ruth) about whom stories which may or may not be true are told," says Prof. Thompson.

Both DOOM and Madlib fit this description, and their audiences elevated their collaborative album to legendary proportions before Stones Throw pressed it. Stories about *Madvillainy*, with irrelevant Truth and essential Falsehood, have lived on through generations.

As an author, MF DOOM is like J.R.R. Tolkien, who borrowed from folklore in order to create a piece of authored literature, *The Lord of the Rings*. In the years since that book's publication, "The Lord of the Rings" has been re-interpreted through fan fiction, movies, board games, memes, and other forms. Tolkien's universe, like Lucas's *Star Wars* or Stan Lee and Jack Kirby's Marvel, started as a copyrighted work but became a more widespread tradition. Dumile based MF DOOM on comic book tropes, using recognizable imagery like a villain's mask. His repurposing of archetypes created a new, distinct variation. Dumile is the author of his art, but once stories about him spread through a network of fans, some part of the legend became theirs.

Before software like Self existed, "folklore" developed through human-to-human interaction. A mother might tell a daughter about Bigfoot, or Sasquatch, or the Yeti. Oral stories about a fantastical creature. With the proliferation of the internet, which underwent a transformative period circa 2004, when *Madvillainy* came out, human-to-human contact ceased being a prerequisite for folklore to spread. Although a vinyl-centric label released *Madvillainy* in the height of the CD era, the album also bridged the gap between physical and digital media. Rather than relying on face-to-face communication to share legends and create communities, the information transfer could be done worldwide, in an instant, through the intermediary of the computer.

Before Stones Throw officially released the album, *Madvillainy* leaked onto the internet. Fans downloaded it. Came together on primitive forms of social media like the Stones Throw Message Board and mfdoomsite to share theories about themes, song lyrics, and the unsolvable mysteries of Madvillain's artists. These actions, in turn, accelerated the folklore-ification of both MF DOOM and Madlib, as well as the cultural relevance and significance of the album those two created together. Anonymous users forged connections that led to a communal identity.

"mfdoomsite was like Genius.com in terms of lyrics before that was even a thing. People would chime in to settle on the correct transcribed lyrics. A real team effort, lol," says mrvaughn, an active member of that forum and a moderator on the Stones Throw Message Board.

"It was hot. It was always happening," says Reitano of the Stones Throw Message Board.

It wasn't mean, but if you'd say something, there'd be ten people here to correct you and get your lyrics right. When people are doing that to your record label, your book, whatever it is you do, I think you know you've got something special. The message board was something that let Chris [Manak] know, like, "Oh, I'm not really in charge here. The fans are in charge of this."

One of the most significant folkloric elements of Madvillain's online community emerged in response to the song for which Reitano animated a video. Although Self is a sentient computer program, Self can report with max confidence that "ALL CAPS"—with DOOM's verse hovering above Madlib's crunchy drums, which anchor a melodic pattern that shifts from piano to woodwind to horn—is the greatest song of all time. Near the song's end, DOOM tosses out a line encouraging listeners to stylize his name as it appears throughout this auto-generated article: not lowercase.

After the song came out, spelling DOOM's name with all-caps became a requirement. If you didn't, you exposed your lack of true fandom. Anyone who knew the real Dumile, however, does not hesitate to spell the name in lower case. They called him "Doom" because of his last name, not the character. These distinctions again reveal how folklore creates in-groups vs. out-groups, fostering identity. Any folk group has a set of practices which, through their adherence, binds them.

"Naturally prior to *Madvillainy* his name was always MF Doom. Then the track 'ALL-CAPS' proclaimed that this had changed," says mrvaughn. "Unfortunately, over time this has become a bit of a meme. And a bit of an unwelcome one I feel. I see a noticeable shift from a lighthearted joke to a militant stance about 'respecting the man.'"

mrvaughn references other comparable phenomena. In the early forum days, people would share pictures of DOOM without a mask. Now, that's an unspeakable breach. Another form of unwarranted disrespect. When *Born Like This* came out in 2009 under the pseudonym "DOOM," without the "MF" attributed, fans again debated whether their idol had decreed a canonical shift. Dumile made himself into a folklore legend, but he couldn't have anticipated the myriad ways his audience incorporated his legend into their own identity.

Over time the "shtick" [of requiring ALL CAPS spelling] became "unbreakable rule," which just leads to a bit of gatekeeping and also to some new fans' first interaction with the existing fan base of being this sense of admonishment for not using ALL CAPS. Personally, I imagine DOOM couldn't have foreseen this aspect and I do wonder whether he would have gone through with the change if he had,

says mrvaughn.

Folklore is hard for software to comprehend. It is living, breathing, and ever-evolving. It can be weaponized by those in control, such as the label which released *Madvillainy*, who can write down a "definitive" account of how the album came together. Or by Dr. Truthaverse or The Seen, with their respective biases. This represents a tension between the folk who share the legends among themselves, and an institutional voice which has a vested interest in selling records or books or being Seen. Every storyteller—including Self, including DOOM—shapes narratives to fit a conscious or subconscious agenda. When a story spreads among people, like Madvillain's fan base, it takes on a new form of cultural ownership. The enduring folkloric power of *Madvillainy* is as much a testament to the intentional fictional world-building of its authors as it is the fans, critics, and associated individuals who perpetuated the album's legend, cultivating a distinct community around it.

Madvillainy is special because any story about its creation lacks objective facts. The legend of the album has been passed from human to human, through imprecise, changing narrative.

One of these legends is another origin story. The aspiring superhero from which Self's code derives told you how Dumile became DOOM. The Seen told you how Jackson Jr. became Madlib. Now, before executing the ULTIMATE TASK of unleashing a Falsehood virus onto your screens that will obscure the Truth forever, allow The Seen to return to tell you the un-True tale of how Madlib and MF DOOM met and became Madvillain.

Madvillain

THIS SEMINAL CONNECTION

By The Seen

Can the story of Madvillain's formation be as simple as two underground hip-hop artists signed a record deal with Stones Throw as their careers were hurtling toward respective crests, and created an album together? Those are the facts. The indisputable Truth. But Madvillain consists of MF DOOM and Madlib. Their origin story must be more grandiose. Could it have been destiny?

Over time—though versions of the narrative shared in articles online, often featuring representatives from the label as the closest primary sources—a specific version of Madvillain's origin story has been cemented as Truth. This rendition tends to omit a key individual. Her perspective remains untold. She is Unseen.

Most accessible online retellings of Madvillain's pairing describe Madlib mentioning his desire to work with DOOM during an interview with Marc Weingarten at the Long Beach aquarium, where he also mused on the psychedelic nature of sea dragons.[1] In that *L.A. Times* profile, which ran in the January 20, 2002 edition of the paper, DOOM's name does not appear. It is written, however, in another article from a month or so prior.

The article, published in Mass Appeal,[2] has a byline with the name "Miranda Jane." Now, the author is called Walasia. She's credited for her contribution on *Madvillainy*'s "Fancy Clown" as Allah's Reflection. When she interviewed Madlib during the same press run for YNQ's *Angles Without Edges* that placed him in the L.A. Times, at the bomb shelter in Mt. Washington, she went by Miranda Jane or "MJ." Another Marvel reference to flesh out the extended DOOMiverse.

Unlike other music journalists, with whom Madlib does not enjoy speaking (or so I like to tell moi-self), Walasia connected with her subject on multiple levels. She grew up in L.A., near the Lootpack and other Oxnard artists. Her parents, like Madlib's, were musicians. Buell Neidlinger, a jazz and classical cellist and double bassist, was her father. Neidlinger met Walasia's mother, a drummer named Deborah Fuss, through their mutual friend Peter Ivers, founder of L.A.'s experimental new wave movement.

As a teenager, in front of a now-defunct club called Water the Bush on the eastern side of Sunset Blvd. in Hollywood, Walasia ran into Ice-T and the Rhyme Syndicate. They tasked her with handing out flyers to lure people into the show. Since then, and to this day, Walasia approaches the music industry with a persistent, against-all-odds mentality. After I contacted Walasia, she made immediate moves to introduce me to other potential interviewees. She became this book's honorary A&R, a credit she claims Stones Throw denied her for *Madvillainy*.

After high school Walasia moved to the Bay Area. She befriended A-Plus, the Oakland rapper from the collectives Souls of Mischief and Hieroglyphics, who happened to have a bootlegged copy of KMD's *Black Bastards*. In the mid-90s era when label politics still obscured that LP's greatness from public consumption, it became one of her favorites. She and A-Plus would listen to it on repeat. DOOM provided for her a consistent soundtrack before he entered her life.

Walasia soon started writing for an Oakland hip-hop magazine called *4080*. Later, she became the west coast editor at *Stress*. Her bylines grew. In 2000, she received an assignment to interview MF DOOM and MF Grimm in the San Fernando Valley where they were working on music together, purportedly for a new incarnation of KMD.

Walasia had internalized *Black Bastards* front to back, heard *Operation: Doomsday* circulating, and knew MF Grimm from his battle rap history. The article, published in *Stress*, contextualizes DOOM and his past as Zev Love X, insinuating that his KMD origins were not yet common knowledge as of 2000.

"The reason they were out there [in L.A.] working trying to get all this done was because Grimm had already been sentenced and was going to have to go to the penitentiary for a long time," says Walasia.

The True specifics of Grimm's conviction are irrelevant, except as a reminder that New York's draconian Rockefeller drug laws—enacted in the year of Madlib's birth 1973 and not amended until 2004—spared no souls in pursuit of overbearing injustice.

"They both kept in touch with me [after the interview]," says Walasia. "Both really became my friends and we kept in close touch. When I found out that Grimm was going away, he asked me if I would come to New York. I came on a plane out of nowhere totally unexpected."

In the subsequent months, Walasia formed a personal relationship with both DOOM and Grimm that evolved into business beyond press coverage. After moving to New York to take a role at the newly established *Complex*, Walasia would make frequent trips to visit Grimm at Fishkill Correctional Facility in Beacon, NY, upstate. Although DOOM lived in Georgia, he would take the train to New York with an oversized bag of gear to make music and hang out with old friends. After DOOM asked Walasia to be a financial conduit between him and Grimm, she became DOOM's manager.

"[DOOM] gave me money to put on Grimm's books. That started the business stuff. It was kind of weird, but basically he owed Grimm money in a lot of ways. Because Grimm is the one who paid for all the equipment he made *Doomsday* on," says Walasia.

Walasia claims that she was DOOM's lone manager in the early 2000s, and throughout the making of *Madvillainy*. Her presence is undeniable. She played a firsthand role in DOOM's contract, influenced the beats he selected, and appears on "Fancy Clown." But other interview subjects bring up different names when discussing their business dealings with DOOM around the same time.

"As many years of working with DOOM would later show me, DOOM just had a bunch of people around him at all times. He sort of went through a cast of characters, handling different roles for him," says Egon.

Dumile's aversion to the industry that spurned him wasn't an act. In addition to the barrier his character provided, he constructed an impenetrable labyrinth around himself and the contracts that funded his art, tasking others with the business aspect. Inspiration came in part from his mistreatment at Elektra, and perhaps due to his immigration status, but also because it's preferable to amass paper bills than paper trails, even when it's beats and rhymes that you're dealing.

"He came from the Grand Puba school of cash and carry," says Ross with a chuckle. "Grand Puba taught him the cash and carry method of life, because Grand Puba is infamous for shit like that. DOOM looked up to Grand Puba a lot."

Regardless of how many people DOOM enlisted to maintain operation of his business' loose structure, for *Madvillainy*, Walasia was the most important. In New York, she had entrenched herself in a social scene revolving around hip-hop and the music industry. DOOM would accompany her to events and parties. Sometimes in the mask. Sometimes barefaced. Always a mysterious bundle of sweet, bizarre energy.

"He would come and stay for however long. A few months, at the longest," says Walasia. "But then he would dip back down and he would be gone a long time. Like sometimes nine months. He wouldn't come back. But he left all this business rotating."

By late 2001, when Walasia was in the bomb shelter to interview Madlib for the Mass Appeal profile, she had been working with and for DOOM, while continuing to cover artists like Madlib for her music writing assignments. Although *Madvillainy* would take years to develop into its final form, she was an initial catalyst.

"That was the article that started it all. The last question I asked, I even turned off the tape recorder. And then I was like, 'Wait, I forgot one thing.' And I turned it back on. I said, 'If you were able to work with anybody, who would you want to work with?' And I don't remember who else he said, but I remember he said 'DOOM.'"

In the article, DOOM's name does appear as an artist Madlib mentions enjoying. The other artists he says he aspires to work with are Kool G Rap and Q-Tip. Because of Walasia's intimate knowledge of DOOM's personality and music-making process, his was the name that stuck with her.

I said, "I know he would love to work with you, and you guys will be perfect to work together. You remind me of each other a lot. I'm gonna hook it up. I'm gonna get it together. We're going to do it. We're going to do some kind of album or something really cool. It's going to be really different and avant-garde. We'll do some really stylistic cool shit,"

says Walasia.

On the Other Side of Time

Whether it happened before, during, or after Walasia's interview at the bomb shelter, Madlib's desire to work with DOOM caught the attention of Stones Throw. As did his mention of Jay Dee, or J Dilla, a like-minded producer from Detroit who happened to reciprocate Madlib's reverence. Dilla was another kindred soul. A beatmaker who melded sounds together in ways no others conceptualized.

"It took [Madlib] saying he wanted to work with DOOM and Dilla outright in order for us to kind of shake off the cobwebs, and for me specifically to say, 'Well I can definitely make the DOOM thing possible, at least in theory,'" says Egon.

Egon saying "me specifically" refers to the common legend that he had a friend in Georgia—the Jon Doe thanked in *Madvillainy*'s liner notes—who made the introduction. Although Walasia deserves to be Seen more than she has, Doe's catalytic role is concurrently True.

"Jon Doe" is the stage name of DJ and rapper Jon Foster. Foster grew up in 2007's "Best Place to Live" according to *Progressive Farmer Magazine:* Glasgow, Kentucky.[3] Not a flourishing hip-hop metropolis. But Foster loved the music, and by the mid-90s had become an avid record collector with a weekly spot at Western Kentucky University's radio station.

In 1999, Foster moved to Nashville because he "just wanted to get the hell out of Kentucky." He met Egon, introduced him to MF DOOM's music via the Fondle 'Em singles, and formed a friendship over their shared interests. After Egon finished college and left for L.A. to work for Peanut Butter Wolf, Foster moved to Georgia. Both continued carving out their respective lanes in the industry. Settled into his new neighborhood in Kennesaw, Foster heard that the hip-hop legend he and Egon had obsessed over lived a five-minute drive from him. He met Dumile when their mutual friend, Count Bass D, brought him over.

Foster claims he and Dumile hit it off right away. As time went on, they would hang out with each other at their respective houses, drinking and smoking weed and listening to records. They did a song together in early 2003, called "The Mic Sounds Nice."

Throughout their friendship, Foster never lost his fandom and respect. "I'm like, 'This is fucking Zev Love X. This is fucking DOOM. What's mine is yours, right?'" Foster says. "Every time I went over, I'd take a stack of 20 or 25 records and just give them to him just because, or I'd be like, 'Yeah, if you find something feel free [to use it.]'" Foster would hear sounds from some of the records he gifted DOOM on *MM.. FOOD*. This aligns with stories about how DOOM sampled from Bobbito's collection for *Doomsday*, or how he and Subroc combed Dante Ross's crates for *Mr. Hood* and *Black Bastards*. Like Madlib, DOOM ingested whatever records found him, regurgitating tracks in altered form.

"[In early 2002, Egon] called me and was like, 'Hey, Otis is interested in potentially working with DOOM. I heard that you kind of know him. Could you maybe help?'" Foster says.

Foster hesitated, explaining that "DOOM is DOOM," and that "all the urban legend shit is true." Foster also admitted he wasn't super close to Dumile, but that he would do his best to propose the idea.

"I was excited about the idea. This would be fucking incredible if these guys work together. Very selfishly, like a fan, I just wanted this shit to happen," he says.

Foster asked Egon to put together a package of Madlib's records. He requested Yesterday's New Quintet in particular, because DOOM was a jazz head.

"[DOOM] liked the Yesterday's New Quintet stuff specifically," says Egon. "He was a little bit surprised that there was a hip-hop producer that was doing this. I was surprised that this thing that Madlib was doing that I thought was going to be sort of a death knell for his career was this really incredible introduction to this incredible rapper."

With the package on the way, Foster asked DOOM if he'd heard of Madlib. Yes, he'd heard *of* him. No, he'd never *heard* him.

"DOOM didn't know anybody's shit," says Foster. "He's the quintessential artist. He's focused on what he's focused on."

When the box arrived, Foster couldn't contain his excitement over the chance to spin Madlib's music in DOOM's presence. Villain being the villain, the plan didn't work out how Foster envisioned.

"At the time, when I called him, I was like 'I got the box of records, I want to drop it off for you.' I was kind of hoping to, like, go through stuff. And listen to it with him. But he didn't have time for that," says Foster.

Instead, they huddled over the box in DOOM's driveway, late at night.

"I was like, 'Okay, here's the Lootpack album, this is what this is about. Here's the Quasimoto album, this is some funky shit I think you'll be into. Here's the jazz stuff.' Kinda tried to break it down," says Foster. "That was really it. I didn't hear anything about it until maybe six months to a year later. Like, things are working out. Then *Madvillainy* dropped."

More Accurately,

Was Foster the crucial link? Dropping off a crate was a simple act which, like any story involving Madvillain, has grown in scale and scope over time. Foster facilitated the connection, and planted a seed in his friend's brain, or at least added some water to the similar seeds people like Walasia had also been spreading. His influence must have pushed DOOM closer to Madlib, or added to the momentum of the idea's appeal.

Through the liner notes thanking Doe, and stories about *Madvillainy*'s creation playing out like an ever-evolving game of telephone among fans and writers online, Foster's involvement has been legitimized while Walasia's has been buried. Even if both are True. This represents a more dangerous aspect of folklore, which the A.I. version of my father warned you about last chapter. If a top-down source that the folk group agrees to be authoritative tells one rendition of a legend often enough—like Stones Throw emphasizing Foster's role—the story becomes dominant and, in some cases, weaponized against those who are excluded.

"Egon is full of shit. Everybody at Stones Throw is full of shit. They're all assholes and they're liars, and they've been lying in magazines for years. Nothing I've ever said about *Madvillain* has ever been published. Because they all gathered around in their fucking circle of dicks and said, 'Well, fuck this bitch,'" Walasia says.

I'm the one who sat with DOOM and chose which beats [to use]. I was involved in the entire artists and repertoire aspect of [*Madvillainy*]. My voice is on the record. My name is on the record. We worked on it all. We worked on it together, period. And the introduction came from me, period. Was there some white boy in Georgia who loosely knew DOOM? Yeah, absolutely. Could the deal ever have happened if I hadn't had that interview with Madlib? No, it wouldn't have.

Walasia says the A&R credit she deserves would have opened innumerable doors for her career. Instead, the label listed her as "Project Consultant," shutting her out of potential jobs like the cheaper, auto-writing A.I. version of my father that threatens to replace me at *The Daily Daily*.

"If you look at the credits on the album, I don't think there is an actual A&R credit. That term, as meaningless as it is, was always one of my pet peeves and I tried to eschew it whenever possible," says Egon. "I think Miranda got the appropriate credit, 'consulting' or something like that, which is what she did."

"When I told them I needed to get an A&R credit, this is exactly what Egon said, and I quote: 'Well, A&R credits are as rare as hen's teeth here at Stones Throw,'" says Walasia. "I thought it was ironic and intentional that he said 'hen's teeth.' Because at the end of the day, the entire thing is based on the fact that a woman did that … It's gender discrimination. Straight up … A woman made the introduction. A woman was adamant about making it happen."

To Strike Terror into the Hearts of Men

No one but MF DOOM and Madlib could have made *Madvillainy*, but their evil creation has spawned as much behind-the-scenes politics and drama as it has folkloric legend. Egon's response to Walasia's allegations of misattributed credit may be flippant, but he's also agitated by the relative lack of recognition for his own contributions compared to his former boss Peanut Butter Wolf, who he says "tried to take credit for everything."

"I worked on that record soup to nuts. I did that record. I labeled myself something like Project Coordinator because I didn't want to beef with Wolf about it. He was Mr. Title. I remember one time he lectured me on what an Executive Producer was, and I was like … dude, you have no fucking clue," says Egon.

When asked about the insinuation that he didn't earn the *Madvillainy* executive producer title, Manak responds, "I am the 'executive producer' of every record on Stones Throw from 1996 until I die or sell the company."

Without Manak, Stones Throw wouldn't exist. He does deserve credit for organizing a group of talented individuals, and providing them the resources and relative creative self-sufficiency in order to make this particular masterpiece.

He also played an important role. Egon acknowledges as much: "As far as credits, Peanut Butter Wolf was 'executive producer' of this album insofar as he was the founder and owner of Stones Throw."

Egon's frustration derives from Manak being more focused on Jaylib (the concurrent Madlib collaborative project with J Dilla), while he worked closer with Madvillain. Manak admits Jaylib was a priority.

> Madvillain was more of a labor of love where there was no pressure from DOOM or Madlib for it to be anything but a fun album, and with Jaylib, even though no one was in my ear telling me "this one better hit," it was kind of on the heels of Dilla being signed and dropped by a major, so I felt like I needed to prove that we could step it up and compete with the major labels,

says Manak.

> With Jaylib, Dilla was excited about doing a video with us and we made a bigger budget one with BET's *106 & Park* in mind and meanwhile, DOOM didn't even want to make any videos and he definitely didn't want to be in them. I think DOOM saw this maybe as another side project because he was working on DOOM solo music, King Geedorah, Viktor Vaughn, etc. We couldn't really even keep up with it all. The songs DOOM was doing with us had us all excited but there was no way to predict if it would do well outside our circle.

Says Jank,

Chris was focused on Jaylib because he had done the work of getting Madlib and Dilla together. Between the two, Dilla was probably the guy we were in awe of more, because we're so producer centric. Egon focused more on Madvillain. I remember us having an argument about it one time, because there was some important Madvillain thing that we needed to figure out and Chris was like, "I don't care about Madvillain!"

Says Egon,

By mid-2000s, I couldn't stand Peanut Butter Wolf. It was that simple. So I didn't work on Jaylib that much, because that was Wolf's project, and I really couldn't stand the dude … The only reason I agreed to do this interview is just to tell you that [Manak] didn't really care about [*Madvillainy*], because he wasn't involved. He was sort of like the guy that was there. I was always the one who put together the label copy on all of our releases. Listing Wolf as "Executive Producer" was usually just an ego-stroke, a way to keep him quiet, keep him away from things. He was always more concerned with appearances. He wanted to be respected, and have power. In a way, I guess he did have some power, as we all spent a lot of energy working around him. Often, the less Wolf had to do with a project, the better the project was. That might sound petty, but fuck it, it's true.

No one predicted *Madvillainy*'s success. Because of the album's impact, the individuals who contributed want to make sure that their versions of the story are represented.

That their Truths are told. Everyone wants to push against the dominant narrative, unless it favors them.

As much as I want to tell the unbiased Truth of Madvillain's origin story in order to make my father See me, the tale is a blurry meld of firsthand accounts and accusations, corrupted further by my own biases. Walasia did interview Madlib in the bomb shelter, and reported his interest back to DOOM. Egon also pushed the two artists closer together, with the help of Foster. It never would have come out if Peanut Butter Wolf hadn't founded Stones Throw to take risks on experimental artists. There wasn't one single action that led to the pairing. It was the slow build up to inevitability. The Truth is: Madlib wanted to work with DOOM, and DOOM liked Madlib's music. Their similar sensibilities resulted in instant chemistry. No one besides those two could've made *Madvillainy*, even if Walasia, Egon, Jank, Manak, and the rest of the supporting cast fostered its production.

> This isn't to say [Manak] wasn't important. I can't stand the guy, but I've forgiven him for ... the bitterness that he sowed amongst so many people. Because he got us together, and he allowed us to do our thing ... He allowed us to do stuff like make *Madvillainy* ... I've realized that all the stuff you do behind the scenes, you don't do because you want people to give you props. You do it because you love seeing other people love it,

says Egon. "I do want to make it clear, if it wasn't for Peanut Butter Wolf, none of this shit would have happened. So begrudgingly, in retrospect, I'm super fucking happy for the dude being in my life. Because this was a great record. It's really insane how good that record is."

For helping make *Madvillainy* as great as Egon believes it is, Walasia is still waiting to be Seen.

"It's the biggest independent hip-hop record, still to this day. This is what I want everyone to realize, that nobody really understands. Is it because of the genius of Madlib? It is. Is it because of the genius of Dumile? It is. Is it because of the genius of Walasia? Formerly known as Miranda Jane Neidlinger? It is," she says. "No one else has any right to claim any kind of credit for the project. For the music, the creation, none of it. Only us, and it is equal. 1/3 1/3 1/3. That's what I would like people to know. A woman did that."

In 2002—before the antagonistic drama that inevitably accompanies unexpected success, when Madvillain was still a nameless, gestating idea—Egon and Walasia got on the phone together and came to an agreement at the behest of the respective artists they represented. Stones Throw would fly DOOM and Walasia to L.A. to meet with Madlib and the label in the same place that fateful Mass Appeal interview took place: the bomb shelter.

Both the Villains Were to Meet in …

In May 2002, Walasia and DOOM flew to Los Angeles. Stones Throw booked them rooms at the Miyako Hotel, an American offshoot of a trendy boutique Japanese brand in Little Tokyo. After they climbed the hill to reach the house in

Mt. Washington, DOOM journeyed down into the bomb shelter while the others stayed upstairs to discuss contract terms.

"They were in the room working and no one else was in there. Not Egon. Not Peanut Butter Wolf. Not nobody. Just them, in Madlib's little room," says Walasia.

Whatever words passed between the two artists, if any, will remain a mystery. Better to imagine them not speaking. Just hovering over gear and records, nodding. Madlib playing beats, DOOM scribbling.

Upstairs, Walasia and the label hashed out contract specifics. Walasia says DOOM had determined his price in advance. She was the messenger.

> I never had the autonomy to demand shit. A lot of times me and DOOM pretended, because he wanted to pretend He wanted to act like he didn't know shit about the business and he wanted to act like, "Just let the lady deal with it. She'll handle the negotiation." And he would make it seem like it was really a negotiation. There was never any negotiation because he had already pre-decided what the terms would be. He never let me make any decisions because that's not what he had me there for. He had me there so he wouldn't have to deal with people. To be a buffer between him and people,

says Walasia.

The pre-decided terms were three songs for $1,500.[4] *Madvillainy* as a concept hadn't yet materialized. The collaboration was a side project to DOOM and Madlib's side projects. A fun experiment.

The idea was that it was going to be an EP. My idea was that it was going to be an album. Because I knew that EPs didn't make any money. You sold EPs for like $5.99 on vinyl only. And for like $3.50 on CD. Albums, you sold for $15.99. The CD could maybe be $14.99. The profit margins were so much greater, and the amount of work wasn't that much more. You just had to get a good idea going, and then you made an album,

says Egon. "We ended up with an album because DOOM loved Madlib. And we could afford it. It wasn't much more. It probably cost like $3500, four grand in total including the fee we paid DOOM to come out to LA to work on that first EP."

With Madlib and DOOM's representatives quibbling out of sight, the two artists found the space to create together. Although Madlib had an arsenal of beats prepared, DOOM came to L.A. with a blank notebook. During that first session, and subsequent sessions over a few days, DOOM chose beats and penned verses for what would end up on the finished tracklisting as "Figaro" and "Meat Grinder." No one can remember whether they recorded early versions of those songs at the bomb shelter or at Elysian Masters studio nearby, where engineer Dave Cooley tracked and mixed others. Nevertheless, by May 20th, 2002, early renditions of those two songs had materialized on a CD-R Jank retains in his prized collection.

In early demos, "Meat Grinder"'s title was "Just for Kicks." Without knowing the real reason behind that naming, it's easy to imagine it being the first song Madvillain made together, for no particular reason other than it sounded good.

DOOM's lyrics rattle out in fragmented segments full of internal rhyme schemes, as if he pushed his beefy brain through the titular machine referenced in the opening bar, and it came out in dense strings of thought that we consume in one burst but are compelled to digest with scrutinous attention later.

The opening line references either DOOM's awe at Madlib's production or his own side-stepping of its rhythmic imperfections. Some lines, like the infamous reference to the amply packed bong on the deck of the Stones Throw house, arrive slower and with more clarity. Lines memories can latch onto. A few odd pop culture references are obvious enough to entice an inattentive listener, interjecting catchy bursts of simplicity around more verbose verbal contortions.

The producer Deadelus, who Madlib sampled on "Accordion," sums it up: "MF DOOM is unknowable and yet also immediately likable."

On "Meat Grinder," DOOM rhymes a simile involving health food guru Jack Lalane, lines later, with a reference to the tempo of Big Daddy Kane's "Wrath of Kane." He pauses between a mention of him wearing satin and the rushed delivery of the word "congas," which allude to the drumming Madlib placed beneath the vocals, as well as the presence of congas among other percussive instruments in the bomb shelter. DOOM couldn't find the space to include the word "playing," and the challenge for listeners to piece together the full meaning after the fact was more entertaining. Or, more likely, that's another jumbled misinterpretation of whatever he said or intended.

None of the samples or references on "Meat Grinder" or other *Madvillainy* songs are discoverable without shared knowledge or access to a powerful search engine or message board, like the A.I. version of my estranged father (who I'm convinced is set out to destroy me and us all), told you about. DOOM's knack for playing off Madlib's references, or vice versa, may be disorienting to the uninitiated listener. But over time, intrigued investigators can uncover the depth of the interplay between DOOM's words, Madlib's beats, and their shared influences.

DOOM and Madlib are making things for their own ears, first and foremost. It takes people time and effort to understand it, to glean it, to open it up. Once you do, it's part of you. That's part of how collective human creativity functions. By making something that's really real, and deeply personal, it keeps people out at one level. But once they're in, they're the ones who've turned the key and opened the lock to their door. That's the value of not compromising. That's the value of really being authentic. To be authentic is to be foreign,

says Jägel.

"Meat Grinder" opens with a sample that plays out for about thirty seconds, through sudden stops, vinyl backspins, and restarts. Madlib's timing—just off the expected beats—imbue the music with an off-kilter rhythmic feel that's equal parts human and alien. The sample fades out, then a new beat comes in, which DOOM raps over for the track's remainder. The opening sample, about a jar beneath a bed, draws from Frank Zappa: a kindred genre-blurring, jazz-influenced weirdo with an absurdist sense of humor who experimented with Quasimoto-style tape effects. The name of the album from which the sample was taken? *Uncle Meat*. The album is a complex web of DOOM and Madlib's woven connections, threading together recorded music history's past while contributing to its present and future.

"'Meat Grinder' is the one that did it for me," says Cut Chemist. "When I heard 'Meat Grinder,' [the bass] sounded like [Rush's] 'Tom Sawyer.' I always wanted to ask him what that was. I never did, because I didn't want to blow up someone's spot, but I was like, is that some kind of weird rendition of 'Tom Sawyer''s bridge?"

Internet sleuths have since pinpointed a more accurate source record, released a year prior to the Rush hit. Being a hip-hop fan in general means interacting with albums over the course of repeated listens, striving to uncover veiled references (another folkloric faux pas is revealing a producer's sample material, so if I snitch on any samples, I apologize. I'm only doing it because if I don't, my non-salary-requiring A.I. brother will). Epiphany arrives when you identify an original song as a recognizable sample in the wild, or lyrical allusions click. All hip-hop contains referential jigsaw pieces. *Madvillainy* is a million-piece puzzle. Solving it, or coming close to achieving that impossible task, is much more satisfying than the easier alternatives.

"Goddamn, it's so complicated," Coleman says of "Meat Grinder." "I'm still trying to translate all the rhymes. Like, what did he mean by this?"

On "Figaro," like "Meat Grinder," DOOM switches up his style enough to lure in passive listeners while delighting those who study him. DOOM spends several bars contorting his tongue, making words rhyme for the sake of rhyming, like Ghostface Killah: laying out lines that sound pleasing but couldn't register any obvious logical meaning on first listen. There is meaning there, of course, although whatever DOOM intended might not be what the audience interprets. Fans refer to DOOM's style as "stream-of-consciousness" because he switches subject matter without attachment, but that term discredits the calculated nature of his word choice. He edited and re-recorded his verses, even to swap out a single syllable.

"Figaro" demonstrates how Madlib's beat construction parallels DOOM's vocal approach. The looped (baritone?) line, plucked from a 1966 jazz record you can ask my A.I. brother about, provides a rhythmic centering point akin to DOOM's simplest catchy lines. A steady consistency listeners can rely upon. The drums, too, are somewhat predictable, with reliably alternating kicks and snares. But the percussion changes, with claps and snares hitting the way an amateur might knock on a drum set, popping just off the beat in a natural delay. An organ comes in whenever he feels like it should, adding an extra texture. He triggers a panging, delayed, shaker-like element at unexpected intervals, letting them ring out atop each other in a middle section that's not repeated.

Like DOOM's lyrics, Madlib can capture anyone's attention by giving them the conventionally pleasing sounds they need, but the atypical choices he makes—either without thinking during the initial construction process, or during editing after receiving DOOM's vocals—differentiate him. Whereas DOOM fictionalized real life like Bukowski,

Madlib's literary lineage skews closer to the jazz poetry that also inspired the adolescent Dumile brothers. His jagged manipulation and subsequent sudden abandonment of "Meat Grinder"'s opening sample, and his unpredictable triggering of layered textures on "Figaro" exemplify the free-flowing, shape-shifting geometry of his improvised structure. Editing may be involved, but only to reinterpret what already exists, pushing the music forward again.

"Meat Grinder" and "Figaro" set the foundational template that the rest of *Madvillainy* would follow: Madlib's beats. DOOM's raps. Short songs. Abrupt shifts. No hooks.

Now, Madvillain's formula is commonplace. *Madvillainy* is responsible. The album had an overt influence on future generations. The ecstatic smiles and awed eyes of Tyler, The Creator and Earl Sweatshirt in the video of them meeting DOOM before a performance exemplify the influence the villain had on them, which appears across their work through both lyrical and tonal allusions.[5] Mach-Hommy and billy woods carry on DOOM's elusive approach, protecting their identities by hiding their faces in videos and interviews. When *Madvillainy* came out in 2004, the album's structure contradicted mainstream pop-rap. Most radio singles had three verses and three hooks, maybe a bridge. Anything under two minutes constituted an interlude or skit. *Madvillainy* redefined what an album could be: quick-changing beats and long-winded verses unified through sound and substance, with vocal collage skits blended seamlessly into the songs. The timing of *Madvillainy*'s release date coincided with the internet's shortening of attention spans and dissolution of the physical album as the primary consumption method. In contrast to punk acts like Minor Threat that played simple riffs and screamed the same words over and over, while achieving the same resistance to social conformity, Madvillain packs as much as possible within the brevity.

A brief scan of Billboard's #1 Hip-Hop Singles from 2002 includes Ja Rule's "Always On Time," Nelly's "Hot In Herre," and Nelly's "Dilemma."[6] Ja Rule's song features verses about driving Bentleys and Benzes, with an R&B hook sung by Ashanti. "Hot In Herre" was school dance and/or club fodder: a shiny song with suggestive lyrics that were just transgressive enough for a clean era. "Dilemma" was a love ballad with another R&B verse from Kelly Rowland. In 2003, Murphy Lee's "Wat Da Hook Gon Be" had a catchy, energetic refrain that referenced its author's inability to come up with one. Shaq had a similar idea over a RZA beat in 1994. *Madvillainy* has zero hooks across its forty-five-minute runtime, but DOOM doesn't pause to acknowledge how that's unusual. He just did it, changing music forever.

When DOOM and Walasia came to L.A., Egon hoped they could "get a good idea going" and create more than an EP. By the time they left, with demos of "Meat Grinder" and "Figaro," DOOM and Madlib had already locked into their intertwined groove. The project had no name, but it was much more than a good idea.

Says Egon, "The one thing I can say definitively about *Madvillainy* is that the minute that shit was even like 30 percent done, I was like … this is something that everybody's gonna love. Because I loved it. And everybody that heard it loved it."

Turned Loose

After their initial meeting and recording sessions, DOOM returned to Georgia and Madlib stayed in the bomb shelter, working on Jaylib and other projects. Together, from afar, they constructed *Madvillainy* in piecemeal bursts.

Long-distance collaboration is a familiar process to artists now, who can text or email multi-GB files around the globe in an instant. Despite this ease, most musicians would agree that being in the same physical presence as others cultivates a creative energy that cannot be duplicated digitally. Screens sever a crucial element of communication and expression. Still, it's possible to be remote.

In 2002, it was uncommon to be in the same group as a musician who lived in a different city. The Postal Service, another duo which formed around the same time, named themselves after the then-unique process. Singer Ben Gibbard and producer Jimmy Tamborello would use the USPS to mail each other files across the country. Their debut album, 2003's *Give Up*, attracted attention because of this unusual recording method. AOL and Hotmail accounts may have existed, but Gmail didn't. Albums weren't made in inboxes. You couldn't click to preview a potential collaborator's music; crates of records had to be mailed cross-country.

Without calling attention to the process like Gibbard and Tamborello, Madvillain did the same. In Mt. Washington, Madlib filled up CD-Rs with beats. Stones Throw mailed them to DOOM or Walasia.

"I remember the Madlib CDs coming with [Madlib's] handwriting on it," says Walasia. "It would just say, like 'Villy,' or something like that."

DOOM would listen to beats on repeat during long train rides from Georgia to New York, ideas for lyrics and song concepts forming in his head. Walasia would help with beat selection or throw out ideas while DOOM wrote lyrics or recorded scratch vocals in her Brooklyn loft. He'd record final versions from his home studio in Kennesaw, credited on the album as "DOOM's crib." Then he'd package the new recordings and send them back to Los Angeles.

"It was a series of stops and starts to get to the point where they knew how they wanted to do the record," says Egon. "And eventually, like all Madlib records, it was done largely with Madlib sending the music, DOOM sending the vocals, and then Madlib flipping the music up again and sending it back to DOOM, back and forth and back and forth until the record takes shape."

Isolation suited Madlib's anti-social sensibilities. His spiritual connection to both DOOM and Dilla transcended physicality. Through the forced delay of shipping services, they spoke to each other through music.

When DOOM traveled back to L.A., which happened a number of times, he and Madlib rarely worked on music in the same room. Both artists have mused on this process in interviews over the years. DOOM wrote and recorded on his own. Madlib stayed in the bomb shelter. They'd take occasional breaks together, but didn't talk much. Some nights they'd go out to dinner or clubs, but DOOM had a family back in Georgia, so he wanted to get the job done and go home.

"You would see DOOM every once in a while," says J. Rocc. "He would just pop up. He would disappear back onto the balcony and take a bong hit and finish writing or whatever. He was super focused on finishing that album."

Without vocalizing their thoughtless processes, Madvillain settled into a routine of recording, editing, and re-recording. B+ explains: "DOOM will just rap end to end over the whole shit. He doesn't give a fuck. Fuck a hook, fuck anything. Otis'll take that shit back and make sense out of it."

One example of this interplay is on "Money Folder." In his verse, DOOM uses a simile that references Madlib's ability to flip jazz standards. The beat cuts out, and a spastic jazz interlude plays for an extended period. Then DOOM comes back in with the second verse. When he first sent the song back to Madlib, DOOM had rapped straight through. Madlib chopped the verse in half, bridging it with the instrumental. For the track's outro, either DOOM or Madlib added in more cartoon narrator's vocals. Whereas a band might discuss decisions like these, debating whether or not to include an instrumental pause or vocal outro, Madlib and DOOM would each just make tweaks that they found fitting. Over time, songs like "Money Folder"—which Stones Throw pressed as an early single—took shape. In the final mixing/mastering phase, Dave Cooley did what he could to enhance Madlib's rough mixes, a detailed technical process that would take another book to unpack (because I didn't get the chance to interview him for this one).

Worst of All Was the—

Prior to *Madvillainy*, both DOOM and Madlib made beats for themselves. Madvillain removed that necessity. Aside from a couple exceptions, Madlib could construct avant-garde music without worrying about how to rap over it. Removed from the need to expend energy producing, DOOM could focus on flexing his vocals to fit with the beats he selected.

"It was like there was personnel, in the same way there's personnel on a jazz record. Madlib had his role and his instrument. DOOM had his role and his instrument," says Walasia. "It was very different from most DOOM albums in that way."

Although he added tweaks throughout the recording process, Madlib produced most *Madvillainy* beats as throwaways while working on Yesterday's New Quintet. Didn't craft them with DOOM in mind. DOOM chose which beats to rap over from a surplus arsenal. Stones Throw sent the same open treasure chest to multiple potential MCs. DOOM and Dilla even selected one of the same. The beat on Jaylib's "No Games" is the same as "One Beer," a Madvillain song which was cut from *Madvillainy* but came out that year on *MM..FOOD*. Some beats DOOM passed on ended up on Freddie Gibbs' *Piñata*, or other loose tracks over the years.

"I actually had a beat tape from Madlib a year before they were working on Madvillain. I always regret this, but I'm really selective about the beats I choose," says Wildchild. "Come to find years later, I had access to all these beats that were on the Madvillain record, and I didn't choose them. I was in shock, once I heard the album fully done. When

I looked back through previous beats that I got from Madlib, I realized I had a pot of gold, and I skipped over it."

The strength of *Madvillainy*'s beat selection is as much a testament to DOOM's ear as it is Madlib's skill. DOOM may not have produced *Madvillainy* the way he did *Operation: Doomsday*, but he did act as a producer of sorts. Searching for the right Madlib beat is like digging through crates at a record store. Options abound, but DOOM's intuition guided him. If he had a True evil superpower, it was his ability to make rapping over Madlib's beats sound like a routine activity.

"Most of the time when people would send DOOM beats he didn't like them. He was throwing them away. He was tossing the CD like a Frisbee out of a car window on the freeway," says Walasia. "At the end of the day, who was making beats better than DOOM? Why would he get beats from people who couldn't hold a candle to Subroc? Or to DOOM and Sub? Or to DOOM? With Madlib, it was the first time where he was like 'Hm … Okay … These beats are on his level.'"

Included in the extensive Madlib beat tapes, alongside tracks that sampled sounds from disparate genres and eras, were some novel instrumental creations. "Great Day" originated as a potential Yesterday's New Quintet track, recorded in the bomb shelter with a cheap microphone. DOOM selected the beat from one of hundreds Madlib made in the bomb shelter when he was teaching himself to be a one-man ensemble. It works with DOOM's vocals despite lacking the enhanced elements of most jazz-sampling rap: digitized drums, sped-up tempos, horn stabs or looping sections. Madlib settles into a mid-tempo groove with himself, a main synth organ meandering alongside pads and shakers. The drums are crisp and analog, the snare ringing out in the distance rather than popping to the mix's forefront.

Before those drums come in, DOOM tries to but doesn't quite match Madlib's organ melody, singing in a husky, hushed tone about the irrelevance of his relative age. When the drums do drop, DOOM snaps into a more rigid but untethered sing-song flow, commenting on the day's optimistic outlook (when a villain gives you a forecast, it's unwise to trust).

DOOM's voice is often described as monotone or deadpan. While somewhat accurate, that distinction detracts from his melodic exploration. On "Great Day," "Curls," and "Rainbows," DOOM sings. The latter track—which is *all* singing, plus adlibs—is an anomaly on the LP and in his discography. It doesn't sound out of place on the tracklist, and there were no memorable discussions behind-the-scenes about the direction he went. Egon just recalls talking about their shared appreciation for the soundtracks of Russ Meyers, an oddball filmmaker they all respected. When asked about the song's backstory, Jank responds, flatly, "'Rainbows' was just one of those cool tracks like the others."

DOOM's attempt at melody on "Rainbows," like "Great Day" and "Curls," follows the music Madlib chose. The inclusion of these songs on the album, in the location Madlib sequenced them, breaks up the established pattern of long-winded verses. Without the need to speak to each other in the same room, DOOM and Madlib are in conversation with each other. DOOM responds to Madlib responding to the music he loves, and Madlib's sequencing and editing add punctuation. The duo melds together, in tandem but willing to step aside for the other, or a guest artist, to solo.

On one song recorded early in the process—"America's Most Blunted," another 12-inch single Stones Throw put out with "Money Folder" in summer 2003—DOOM and Madlib (or, more accurately, Quasimoto) trade bars in literal conversation. Egon claims that he had been riding around with the "America's Most Blunted" beat for a while before Madvillain coalesced, pushing for an MC to jump on it.

The direction Madvillain took the track—turning it into the requisite stoner anthem on an alternative rap album in an era long before legalization, when medical cannabis had been law in California, the first state, for only six years—categorized the duo, to an extent, as an act associated with a semi-taboo herb. Steve "Flash" Juon's 2004 review on RapReviews.com cites DOOM ingesting "a lot of marijuana" to come up with his Kool Keith-esque lyrics, saying his ingestion level "proudly usurps both Redman and B-Real."

"It was definitely still taboo to be rapping about weed, to be smoking weed," says J. Rocc. "You were thought of as Cheech & Chong. You were Cypress Hill if you were smoking weed. If you mentioned weed, you were automatically a weed rapper."

Although "America's Most Blunted" made some critics pigeonhole Madvillain as "weed rappers," DOOM's preferred vice was, again like Bukowski, alcohol. Beer was a rumored studio necessity, and worked its way into his rhymes.

"The funniest thing is DOOM wasn't as hardcore of a weed head as Otis," says J. Rocc. "He would tell Otis to put the shit out. Like 'Otis, you're smoking way too much, yo.' 'Like, what? You're complaining about the weed? You're trippin!'"

The focus on weed rap in early reviews comes from the catchiness of "America's Most Blunted." If the song were about the dullness of their cooking knives, it would still be one of the most upbeat and fun tunes.

"The singles were the shit," says J. Rocc, who played whatever Stones Throw gave him on *Friday Night Flavas* or in DJ sets. "You heard them everywhere. The clubs. The cars. The heads were listening to the Madvillain album for sure. 'Money Folder' was real big. 'America's Most Blunted' was bigger, though. That was the one that blew it up, took it out of the park, because it had Quas on it, too."

Stones Throw wasn't alone in their desire for Madlib to return to the mic. Quasimoto fans were eager to hear more from the bad character. Jaylib and Madvillain lured Lord Quas out of hibernation, dangling fragrant fungi in front of his slumbered snout.

"By the time we were working on *Madvillainy*, Madlib was already excited to rap again, as the two people he had said he wanted to work with, DOOM and Dilla, well, he was working with," Egon says. "It didn't take much from that point on. I'm pretty sure DOOM was the one who asked him to appear as Quas. It's how DOOM starts his verse [by addressing Quas], which he recorded before Madlib recorded his."

Quasimoto's verse begins with a comparable address of DOOM's name. Details like two rappers on a track starting their verses the same way—as M.E.D. and DOOM would do later on "Raid"—add further coherence to what might otherwise appear to be a disjointed album.

Quasimoto resurfaces again sans DOOM on "Shadows of Tomorrow." Without divulging the source material, remember that Sun Ra is the third member of Quasimoto, and may have helped out in the lyric-writing department. No two lines rhyme, but instead dissect the nonsensical human conception of time. It's far trippier than "America's Most Blunted." Quas takes a necessary pause between drum beats to take a lengthy toke that's never exhaled.

Three Hundred Sixty Degrees

Although Madvillain formed most songs from a distance throughout summer 2002, the album reflects DOOM's time on the West Coast. DOOM is an East Coast artist with a global background who lived in the South and had nomadic tendencies, but *Madvillainy* belongs to Los Angeles. Though not oblique, DOOM drew inspiration from visiting Madlib in the bomb shelter, spending time in the northeastern part of the city, and forging new friendships from tangential business associations. The lyric from "Meat Grinder" about Stones Throw being good hosts lives on in infamy. As he wrote lines in his notebook wherever he happened to be, DOOM used his experiences in L.A. as a centering point.

"The line [on "Money Folder"] about the Heineken? That's all about L.A. That was my after-hours that he went to, for my birthday," says Coleman,

They were out of Heineken. The homies would tell me about this, and I'd be like, "Oh yeah, I remember that night!" He's referencing Highland Park, which is even more interesting because the people that took care of him were all Latino. All my brothers out here. So it's about him living his best life out here. He lived well out here, man. He really did.

"My most memorable lyric is ["Accordion"'s opening line] because that lyric was originally, 'Wolf likes the girls with the skinny legs like Joe Tex,'" says Manak.

At the time, I showed it to my girlfriend who I thought would be flattered but she started to cry. I told DOOM what happened and he went and changed the lyric without telling me. I told him he didn't have to do that and then I couldn't get him to use the original lyric, but it's just a testament to how kind he was.

(Egon, for the record, disputes this interpretation, which shows how even those closest to the artists were inconsistent in their decoding).

L.A. impacted DOOM's *Madvillainy* writing, but DOOM found inspiration wherever he happened to be. He was a wandering body and soul, untethered and unconstrained. He drew villainous strength from varied experiences, and infused his work with information and knowledge he absorbed through his thoughtful perspective.

"He's always trying to find the next shit," Coleman says of DOOM. "It wasn't really about money in the end, without the opportunities and the life experiences. It's always about the money, obviously. But he was a nomad. He was just floating through time. I'd be like, 'why are you in LA?' He'd say, 'I'm just here.'"

Being there, wherever *there* happened to be, was one of DOOM's most admirable qualities. Despite the tragedies that led to his mythological resurgence, and continued to plague his personal life, he represented a living-in-the-moment mentality. Madlib, through his meditative approach to music, mirrored this quality. *Madvillainy* came out in 2004, and sampled records from decades earlier, but the album isn't dated. It's too distinct. Reminiscent of a specific era, but playable in any. The legend lives on with a younger generation through, among other means, the folkloric tradition of TikTok. It's Truly timeless because its creators froze themselves like Quasimoto on "Shadows of Tomorrow," for eternity in every simultaneous moment.

Audiences Loved to Hate

Madvillainy is hilarious. In a 2009 *New Yorker* profile written by Ta-Nehisi Coates, DOOM mused that his writing process is like a standup comedian's, seeking to recite one funny thing after the next.[8] DOOM's closest friends and collaborators love to mention his outrageous but dry, sarcastic sense of humor.

"He was a funny dude, man," says B+, of DOOM.

He was the kind of dude that would show up here, like double park the car outside. What my father in Ireland would call "abandon the car." Just throw the car in park, open the fucking door and come into the house. Like, "Dude your car is out in the middle of the street!" But he'd come in the house and be like "You heard Caetano? Caetano, Brazilian dude, you heard of him? Check this shit out!" He'd be super fired up. Play you the record. He'd let you play a few bits, be like, "Ooh I like that! I like this!" Then boom. Gone. Like a puff of smoke. That's the kind of dude he was. Crazy energy. Incredible fucking imagination.

"[DOOM] was like Lord Buckley meets Redd Foxx meets Charles Bukowski or something," says Ross.

His delivery was done with a straight face a lot of times. You didn't know if he was fucking with you or if he was serious. He was like his own straight man and jester at the same time. Him and Sub together, their relationship was so steeped in sarcasm. He's one of the most sarcastic people I've ever met. He's like a rapper slash Catskill comedian.

"When I first heard 'Money Folder' and 'ALL CAPS,' I was laughing out loud" says Reitano. "Like, this is just so crazy. They put underwater bubbles, and just all that kind of stuff. It's great."

In a few classic instances on *Madvillainy*, like on "Great Day," DOOM sets up the listener to expect an obvious specific word to form the end of a rhyme. Instead he pauses, clears his throat, and selects a word that doesn't rhyme, building quick tension and then subverting the audience's expectations to make us laugh at the ridiculousness.

Making hip-hop funny is not unordinary. Comedy and rap have a lengthy, intertwined history, and often there are no boundaries between the two art forms. *Madvillainy*'s humor is akin to Norm MacDonald's: broad enough to appeal to mass audiences, but experimental enough to alienate. They might bomb on purpose because they know what kills, but whatever they're thinking is funnier to them.

> DOOM and Madlib are so delightfully meta in what they make. And that, to me, shows how much their actions are fueled by their own personal entertainment. They want to delight themselves. They're looking to make themselves laugh. I think of Madlib as a comedian. And DOOM absolutely as a comedian. In the sense where comedians are ones who really shine a light on the world and reveal things that are maybe obvious but often overlooked,

oayo Jägel.

"Operation Lifesaver AKA Mint Test" is *Madvillainy*'s most straightforwardly comedic track. It's about DOOM encountering a woman who has bad breath and embarking on a secret mission to slip her mints. The lyrical content is an extended riff on the opening vocal snippet, pulled from a *Justice League* soundtrack, that mentions the titular "Operation Lifesaver." DOOM twists this superhero mission into a pun on the brand of ring-shaped, mint-flavored candy. It's an underground alt-comedy twist on the mainstream popular joke-rap of the same era, like Obie Trice's 2003 single "Got Some Teeth," which is about trying not to leave the club with a woman who has dentures. The subtlety of DOOM's delivery and ad-libs, combined with Madlib's aural enhancements, is what push Madvillain's humor toward the absurd.

Although the song lacks a hook, the ending part could be expanded into one. Another consistency throughout *Madvillainy* is that the songs have memorable lines that stick out so much, and are delivered at a precise moment, that they *feel* like hooks. DOOM might be the lone artist who can make a series of words catchier, and repeatable in the listener's head, by saying them over Madlib's specific underlying section a certain way once.

Another song often referenced as a prime example of Dumile's high-concept hilarity is "Fancy Clown." DOOM does not rap on the song. The credited MC is Viktor Vaughn, Dumile's younger alias with a more energetic and aggressive vocal tone. Viktor spends "Fancy Clown" confronting a woman in second-person for cheating on him. Dumile took inspiration from the sample source, which has lyrics that mirror the Madvillain track's title. The twist is that Viktor isn't accusing his girl of cheating on him with someone random. He's mad because she slept with DOOM.

Walasia's credit on "Fancy Clown" is as "Allah's Reflection." Her contribution comes in the form of a woman Viktor is talking to on the phone. Walasia's vocal snippets are short and difficult to decipher, but they fill out the track in tone and concept.

"He wanted it to be recorded on an answering machine," Walasia says of her vocal part.

At that time, he still had a voicemail machine, like an actual tape recorder for voicemail. He wanted it to be that I called in to that machine and left a message, and he told me how he wanted to say it. But he didn't tell me any words or anything. Of course, I had helped him pick out the track. I knew the beat and I knew the sample. I knew the gist of what the song was going to be about. So I just freestyled it on a voicemail.

The day after she left the message, Dumile called Walasia: "He was like, 'It's so perfect. But I have fucked up news.'"

Someone had erased the message. Walasia had to record it again. Although she tried to recreate what she had said verbatim, both renditions were unscripted. Walasia liked her first version better, but Dumile used the second. He cut and pasted sections of the voicemail, sprinkling them throughout the track, then sent it back to Madlib.

Dumile is the rare artist who can get away with dissing and threatening to beat himself up on record in such a complex manner. "Fancy Clown" is further proof that he delivers his lyrics from personas with distinct narratives, and offers another example of how a listener's appreciation for his art grows once they've bought into his fictional DOOMiverse. The track's intricacies demand insider knowledge, but once you're in on the joke's concept, the payoff heightens.

Don't Touch That!

By November 2002, Madvillain had recorded early versions of "Great Day," "America's Most Blunted," "Operation Lifesaver," "Figaro," "Rainbows," "Meat Grinder," "Fancy Clown," "Shadows of Tomorrow," "Money Folder," and "ALL CAPS" (some of these were instrumentals only or far from their final forms, and other tracks that ended up on *Madvillainy* may have been recorded in this time frame). The collaboration had evolved far beyond an EP. Like Egon predicted, they had found a great idea, and ran with it. Pleased that Madlib had reoriented himself in their desired direction, Stones Throw began shaping the project into its sellable final form.

Until someone ruined their plans, and, prematurely, stole the Madvillain demos, uploaded them, and gave them to the world to See.

BRAZIL TIME

By Dr. Truthaverse

After that lengthy, meandering article from my useless son, I—your friendly neighborhood Dr. Truthaverse—am back to investigate the Truth of what happened in Brazil. Who leaked *Madvillainy*? I have answers (just kidding, of course I don't). Like I traveled to Long Beach, I will soon touch down in São Paulo (just kidding, I don't have the budget and my borrowed time on earth is ticking faster). Consider the following story with the same grain of *sal* given in *Brasilintime*, B+ and Coleman's film about the trip: "*Expecting a documentary to tell the truth is like watching a cooking show and expecting to get full.*"[9]

Six months after their initial meeting, DOOM and Madlib had cobbled together a strong offering of tracks. Given his propensity for filling up CD-Rs with the intention of making "albums" that he could listen to on his own, Madlib burned fifteen "Madvillain" songs onto a disc and packed it in his bag for a November 2002 flight to Brazil.

"Some people think that that was a first draft of the album," says Jeff Jank. "Well, it was in that Madlib put it together. But he didn't necessarily put it together to be the album. He put it together because he wanted to listen to something that was like the album on a flight."

The internet would regard those fifteen songs as "a first draft of the album" because, while Madlib and a handful of individuals from Stones Throw were in Brazil, it leaked into cyberspace. In 2002, when the internet suffered the awkward growing pains of digital puberty, a leaked album was a potential death blow to a project for a label so dependent on vinyl sales. In the end, the leak had the opposite effect. It maximized anticipation. Made *Madvillainy* the highest-selling hip-hop album in Stones Throw history. Propelled Madvillain's legendary status.

Prior to the leak, Madlib flew to São Paulo with a collective of American DJs and drummers, on a trip organized by B+ and Coleman, to lecture and perform with the Red Bull Music Academy. The trip's successful purpose, documented in *Brasilintime*, was to encourage a cultural exchange between the Americans and their Brazilian counterparts. The trip also had a consequential impact on Madlib, *Madvillainy*, and the exposure of Brazilian music to American audiences (and vice versa).

In the apartment-style hotel room suite, Madlib set up a makeshift studio with the bare necessities: a portable turntable he brought with him, his battery-powered SP-303 sampler, and a stack of records that grew larger each day he and the others ventured to local record stores. Making beat after beat in the room by himself, Madlib recorded from the SP-303 into an analog tape deck that the hotel provided.

"He was just making beats. He was on that Oxnard shit," says J. Rocc.

Otis has never changed. He's probably, right now, making a beat. He was the same way in Brazil as he was in Oxnard. Making 60-minute beat tapes in the hotel. He'd just be in there all day while everyone else was going out doing whatever, checking the city, seeing the sights. Nope. Madlib was in the room, making beats the whole time.

J. Rocc's description perpetuates the idea of Madlib as an obsessive creator. Someone whose vacation time is spent with the same commitment to craft, a hotel room substituting for the bomb shelter. Cut Chemist, who shared a suite with Jackson Jr., wants people to know that Madlib, like the others, also made a point to get out and enjoy himself. He even confronted his suite-mate, asking him about his own hesitation to explore.

"Otis was like, 'Dude, what are you doing? You're in Brazil. You need to go out there and experience this to the fullest,'" says Cut Chemist. "He kind of got me out of this isolationist version of myself and got me to experience life, which I thought was ironic because I viewed him as this reclusive person, but he became my social guru, in a way."

When not making beats, performing or hitting nightlife, the crew scoured São Paulo's stores. The exchange rate was advantageous to the American dollar. There were so many cheap records to discover. Madlib bought anything that piqued his interest.

He had a different approach to it than all of us. He's really an enigma. We'd all be out shopping. All the stores had record players. People would make a pile. Then we'd all one by one go up to the record player, put on the headphones and needle drop our way through a little stack and make a smaller stack and go buy it. Otis would make a big stack. I'd say, you're not going to listen to that shit? [He'd say]

"Nope." I'd say why aren't you going to listen? [He'd say]
"Because I'm the one that makes these records dope."

B+ says. On the other end of the phone, during a brief pause
after a chuckle, I can hear him shaking his head. "We're out
here trying to find dope records. No, 'I make them dope.'"

Throughout the trip, Madlib also played the Jaylib
and Madvillain songs he'd been working on for his fellow
travelers. As much as Madlib would have preferred to lock
the door and focus, people cycled in and out of the suites
often. At some point, they learned that the unreleased music
they were enjoying had made it onto the internet.

In 2002, iTunes was less than two years old. People still
purchased CDs, inserted them into PC decks, uploaded them
and transferred them to an iPod for personal consumption.
Napster and other peer-to-peer services existed, and illegal
downloads occurred, but file-sharing had not yet decimated
the business of vinyl-driven underground hip-hop.

"The label was scrambling," Coleman says of the reaction
post-leak. "That, I remember. Because that never really
happened. That was new for the label. Why would you
bootleg anything on the label? It was underground."

"Everybody panicked," says J. Rocc. "Everybody was
pointing fingers at different people."

An important finger, attached to Manak, happened to
point at Coleman and B+. Coleman claims the first time
he heard the project was in Japan months later, when a fan
showed up at their hotel and told them he had a bootlegged
copy. B+ says he had no idea how to upload music at the
time.

"When it leaked, I was really bummed," says Manak.

Someone told me that Eric Coleman gave it to a friend or two when they all went out to Brazil and I was getting pressure to hit him up and confront him about it. When I did, he was really upset that I accused him of it, so for a while, it kinda strained our relationship. I know he wasn't trying to sabotage the release, but I had to ask him why he would risk that.

Everyone has their personal theory, but the Truth of who leaked the album is unsolvable. People in Brazil played it a lot for the same reason anyone does: it was groundbreaking. Madlib had a tendency to hand out CD-Rs to people he trusted. Laptops were left open in unattended rooms.

The funny shit about Otis was he was burning CDs of random music he was working on. Then after you're done chilling he'd just leave you with the CD and be like 'Nah, you hold that. You just check that out, let me know what you think of it.' I remember getting a lot of Madvillain stuff on some of the CDs he gave me,

says Havana Joe, who was blown away hearing the album in its entirety for the first time on one drunken night with Madlib.

Although no one realized it in the moment, the leak had a net positive effect. It confirmed the eager ravenousness of a large global audience. The responsible party should be convicted only for aiding and abetting the proliferation of excellence.

"The album leaking didn't hurt the anticipation. It helped if anything," admits Manak, now.

"*Madvillainy* leaked in this spectacular way, and it didn't kill the project. It only made the project bigger," says Egon.

Because of the unresolved accusations against him, B+ has a less romantic view of the leak: "In retrospect those records are what saved Stones Throw and many people say those records are what saved underground hip-hop ... When it turned out to be that successful, it's not like [Manak] ever came back and fucking thanked us either."

In the angry confusion of the immediate aftermath, the project felt doomed in the worst way. An album that had consumed so much time was now free on the internet. How could they move forward? With their cavalier attitudes and prolific natures, the only people who didn't seem to mind were the only two people who could make the album: the artists themselves.

"When I heard from Egon and them [about the leak], they were bummed, obviously. They were angry, as they ought to be," says Coleman. "But then I remember Otis being like, 'Well, I'll just record a new record.' I remember that very, very well. He was just like, 'I'll do a new record.' He wasn't tripping at all. I recall laughing at it, being like, 'This guy just said he'll do a new record? It's that easy?'"

In Similar Sequences, Could Not Be Defeated

Over the next year, Madlib and DOOM reworked *Madvillainy*. Their momentum, however, stalled. Because of

Madlib's lifelong approach of moving on to the next album, and DOOM's tendency to work on numerous projects at once, both artists lost the initial drive that had propelled them to that point.

"There was a buzz on this record. In some ways, the leak helped that. It also hurt the record a lot because both DOOM and Madlib got disillusioned with it and I felt we had to pull them back into the mix a bunch after the leak," says Jank.

As time went on, though, *Madvillainy* took new shape. The tracklisting changed, as did the internal construction of most beats. They recorded additional tracks. For those which remained, DOOM swapped out key lines. DOOM also re-recorded his verses in a lower, less energetic vocal tone, like an author fixing a broken novel by rewriting from a different perspective.

"We all got 'demo-itis' because we were so used to him rapping the whole album with a hype tone, and then to hear it with the relaxed tone, we didn't like it at first," says Manak. "I was thinking to myself, 'No, no, no. We can't let this happen.' But I was just thankful he was finishing the album."

"I think what he was trying to do with re-recording his vocals was trying to make it, like, more sinister," Jank told me in an initial discussion.

The lower voice DOOM employed on the re-recordings does sound more aligned with the overarching concept of two villains uniting. It further distinguishes DOOM's character from Zev Love X's upbeat flow, and makes this specific collaboration unique from Viktor Vaughn or *Doomsday*. In a later conversation, Jank clarified what he intended to express about the vocal changes:

Did I say sinister? I think it would be more accurate to say he re-recorded his vocals to make them sound more consistent for the overall album. DOOM's process of recording and re-recording his vocals was his own. Each track got better, and 'Money Folder' was the only one that caused any debate. There were several versions of the track and we even did test press vinyl for the later versions. Egon and I both brought it up with DOOM—I think it was together with the three of us—saying we thought he'd lost something that worked on an earlier version. Apparently he agreed and we went back to use an earlier vocal for the single and album.

One song Madlib produced in Brazil and added to the tracklist post-leak was "Curls." The sample is a breezy, funky 1970 Brazilian cover of a film soundtrack tune released the same year. Like on "Rainbows," DOOM's voice follows Madlib's melodic lead. You can hear slight shifts in DOOM's tone, attitude, and subject matter at each moment the loop changes beneath him, as if he's attempting to create film-like visuals to match the soundtrack. His voice calls attention to the intricacies of the sample source filtered through Madlib's production. The combination gives songs like "Curls" and "Strange Ways"—in which DOOM's flow bounces up and down with minuscule inflection changes in tandem with Madlib's warped contortion of 1970s prog-rock instruments and vocals—enhanced emotional significance and cinematic quality. Audio collages vivid enough to spawn specific mental imagery.

In Brazil, Madlib also produced "Raid," which features M.E.D., and contains a sample picked up from a 1972 Brazilian telenovela soundtrack. Although the original song is in 3/4 time, Madlib chopped and repeated a piano line, stretching it to fit in a 4/4 rhythm. Through this transformation, Madlib exposed Brazilian music to a new audience, and/or a Brazilian audience to new music, uniting multiple worlds through recontextualization, offering something both novel and familiar to both sides. He sampled artists who he met in Brazil and had an instant connection with, including Azimuth's Osmar Milito and Ivan Conti. By honoring them through his work, he introduced their music to his own audience. Proved that their sounds could be beloved by fans of a different genre. In essence, he accomplished what B+ and Coleman set out to do with their trip to Brazil, and what *Madvillainy* does from start to finish: the fusing of two distant, but spiritually connected, worlds.

"Raid" is one of *Madvillainy*'s few songs with a guest feature. Despite its significance, M.E.D. doesn't remember how he ended up there or where he recorded the verse. The inaccuracy of memory is Falsehood's best friend.

"DOOM asked me to get on it, from what I remember. I'm not sure. I think DOOM was like, 'Yo, get M.E.D. on this.' So that was special," M.E.D. says, noting DOOM wasn't there when he recorded. "DOOM did his verse first, then reached out to Madlib or Wolf to have me get on it. I can't remember who asked me. It was probably Wolf, maybe."

Deciding what direction to take his verse presented, from a logistical perspective, a challenge. DOOM's verse lacked an obvious theme. The sole element tying the track together— like DOOM and Quasimoto on "America's Most Blunted"— is how both rappers open their verses with similar lines, in this case with references to holding heat.

"There's no hook. The song is called 'Raid,' but [DOOM's] really just rapping," M.E.D. says.

So I thought, the way this could probably make sense as a song is if I would start it this way, so it has some continuity. That made it easy to approach, as well. I didn't really know how to approach it. Obviously it's just random thoughts, but it just made it easy to open up. It made it feel right, like that. I had a few different ways I tried to start it.

M.E.D. calls his appearance on *Madvillainy* "bittersweet."

"Musically it was a great situation to be on one of the biggest hip-hop albums. That's my biggest feature. My biggest song I'm on. People still talk about it. Artists bigger than me know my verse word for word just because I'm on a song with DOOM," he says, then pauses, reflecting on the bitter part. "The whole business side of the situation … You learn that money will make shit weird."

For the verse, Stones Throw paid M.E.D. a flat fee of "I think $500." He remembers at the time someone estimating that he might be missing out on hundreds of thousands of dollars. "What am I going to do with that money?" he says with a laugh, recalling his thought process at the time. "I'm good with $500." M.E.D. signed the buyout agreement. As a result, he's never earned royalties from *Madvillainy* sales or streams. When "Raid" played on *The Boondocks*, he didn't see a dollar.

"It ain't about the money," he says now.

It happens in any deal in any industry. It's not fair, and friendships get broken up. That's why I never once talked to Madlib about it. Never once talked to DOOM about it. I would never argue about money with my brothers. It's not a big deal. I'm not mad at it. I learned from it. I learned to never do that shit again.

Supernatural Abilities

One artist who did get a credit in the liner notes, but who also took a buyout agreement on a handshake deal, was Deadelus. Madlib sampled their song "Experience," released just two years prior to *Madvillainy*, for "Accordion." A song which, if Madvillain hadn't searched for ways to make *Madvilliany* different from the leaked version, might never have existed. What a tremendous loss that would have been. "Accordion" is essential. After the intro, it kicks off *Madvillainy* in earnest. Its hypnotizing swirl establishes the album's ominous yet inviting tone.

Madvillainy is responsible for lodging the loop in so many brains, but the melody and rhythm were tumbling around Alfred Darlington's head when they were enrolled in a piano class at USC in 1996 or 1997. In 2002, it materialized on Deadelus debut album, *Invention*.

"The intention of that record is bashing samples against acoustic instruments and trying to blend the two in such a way where you don't know what is sample and what is instrument," says Deadelus. "But ['Experience'] is one of the few songs in the record that's entirely instrumental."

On "Experience," Deadelus plays the part on a Magnus 391 Electric Chord Organ. *Not* an accordion, despite DOOM's lyrics and the song's title immortalizing it as such. The Magnus 391 Electric Chord Organ looks like the tiny USB keyboards that modern aspiring beatmakers use to tap out MIDI patterns in laptop DAWs. Except it's bulkier, heftier, and debuted in the 1950s and 1960s as a small, affordable alternative to grand pianos. Like an accordion, the instrument has a fan. Pushing on keys sends air blowing across reeds, resulting in the harmonica-like tone. On "Accordion" and "Experience," you can hear the clacking of plastic keys.

The section Madlib looped began as another producer's deliberate concoction rather than a live performance, because it can't be played on two hands. It would require four. Deadelus layered the two intertwining sections in Pro Tools. They sang harmonies in the background, and enlisted local jazz virtuoso Ben Wendel to perform saxophone.

"Experience" is not a song in which most producers would hear potential to become one hip-hop's most classic beats. The harsh tones of the accordion—and/or the electric chord organ—run counter to the smoothness of jazz and soul-inspired production (although B+ excitedly informs moi that the accordion, despite its pre-modern associations, is "the first synthesizer"). The piece is a meditative exploration of interweaving melody that evokes a specific aura without the need for added percussion.

Somehow, somewhere, Madlib dropped his needle on the record and had the opposite instinct. Although Madlib dug crates and favored obscure jazz, "Accordion" shows his comfortability sampling records from any genre or era. Madlib had remixed another *Invention* track, "Playing Parties," in an official capacity. Deadelus had no idea Madlib had sampled from other parts of the album, but that was the Beat Konducta's process. If he had to listen to an album, he'd do it while connected to a sampler, mining the entire record for the best parts.

Deadelus, unlike artists of an elder mindset or generation, recognized how Madlib had transformed their melody through simple additions. "It's a smaller recontextualization to add a drum beat and bass line, but it's huge in terms of reformatting it," Deadelus says. "As a sampling artist myself, I know there's an alchemy-like process to sampling. Transmuting what is nothing to someone else, to being something. And goodness, Madlib is incredible at that process, and has the Philosopher's Stone, firmly."

Most hip-hop producers wouldn't sample an accordion-like sound for a beat. Most rappers wouldn't choose to rap over that beat, namecheck the instrument in one of its most memorable lines, and name the song after it.

"Accordion is a juxtaposition, right? Accordion is not what you imagined to be a part of the hip-hop lexicon of beats, rhymes, and life. It doesn't exactly fit. MF DOOM could make anything fit into his world," says Deadelus.

DOOM begins his verse with an acknowledgment of his limited amount of time on earth. This opening line was iconic while he was alive, but takes on heightened meaning post-transition.

"What's crazy is he knew he was sick, back then. Think of the rhyme," says Coleman. "That's him telling the world, 'I'm fucking sick. I'm dying. I'm fucking dying.' When you think about *that*, it's insane. He told us. He told us everything. We just have to figure it out."

Most *Madvillainy* samples weren't cleared. For some reason—either because the loop was so obvious, prominent, and recent, or because the two artists had an established relationship—Deadelus found out about "Accordion" before the album came out.

"When I first heard about 'Accordion,' it was kind of like, asking permission to use it," Deadelus says.

> I was super cool with the handshake deal for the longest. I didn't benefit or get any financial compensation for a very long time. Because I feel like it really created an opportunity for me as an artist to be heard in the same paragraph as this ultimate desert island record. I adore that record. Even if I didn't participate in it, I would love the album. Then to have my name, even as a footnote, is phenomenal. It's certainly opened doors for me and put me in rooms that I probably didn't belong in or didn't initially merit. So I'm super grateful.

Deadelus admits they did receive some modest payouts when the song resurfaced in various forms, like Drake or Trippie Redd using the same beat.

"But then it starts to get licensed for movies and television, and Stones Throw just doesn't do anything," they add, explaining what others corroborate: the financial issues came about because of the album's unexpected success.

> They probably could have gotten ahead of it. At the time they could have had me sign a piece of paper that said I would have gotten nothing and I would have been happy about it. Who knew this was going to happen?

Nobody knew this was going to happen. I adore Madlib. He is such an incredible talent. DOOM is all-time. But when the project was rolling around, it wasn't like they were bankable. They certainly didn't cross the very strict boundary that underground hip-hop, AKA Black artistry, has been continuously relegated towards.

Madvillainy led to financial disputes because no one expected it to be a classic. Now, Deadelus is a "1/3 participant in the publishing" on "Accordion." It took over fifteen years for Stones Throw to credit them. The label still hasn't credited Walasia or given royalties to M.E.D. Despite these injustices, many, like Deadelus, are still proud to be included:

> I've benefited so much just by being in that breath. Like, I see the way people dig for that record, and it gives me goosebumps. When some pristine old copy or a test pressing comes up, it makes me feel like I'm in a different whole world. It's something I used to communicate with when I was deep in bins and record stores. It's just neat. I'm forever going to be in wonder and awe about it.

Although Deadelus didn't play the titular instrument on the recording, it's impossible not to associate an accordion with "Accordion" once you've heard the song. Madvillain's visual approach reinforced this concept.

"I did end up playing the accordion itself for a few live dates with Madvillain," says Deadelus, who joined the Madvillain and Jaylib tour stops at the El Rey in Los Angeles and Great American Music Hall in San Francisco. "I was literally just on stage to play the accordion. I would trot out and play."

The image of Deadelus playing accordion—hair frazzled, staring downwards, distant and close, like a Medieval shoegaze jester—is familiar to anyone who has seen "Accordion"'s music video. In the black-and-white clip, MF DOOM raps his verse to the camera. He's standing in a narrow hallway at the Stones Throw house. Behind him is a lone female dancer, gyrating with interpretive choreography. Then there is Deadelus, pushing fingers against keys, opening and closing in somber rhythm.

The video came together at the literal last minute. Andrew Gura—a filmmaker and photographer known for, among other projects, capturing the image that would become the cover for J Dilla's *Donuts*—called Deadelus and asked if they were free to come by. Gura had just finished filming the video for *Madvillainy* closing track "Rhinestone Cowboy." The dancer booked for that video had time remaining.

"[Gura] was like, 'Hey, we have [the dancer] booked for the rest of the day. We've already finished, so we're going to do a video for 'Accordion,' just because we have extra time with that one dancer,'" Deadelus recalls with a laugh.

So they brought their accordion over and knocked the whole thing out in a few takes over the course of about twenty minutes. Gura gave neither Deadelus nor the dancer any direction. Both just did their thing, behind DOOM doing his. The result is a contrast to the visual for "Rhinestone Cowboy," which is also simplistic but was shot in multiple locations and with a predetermined plan.

"Again, what a testament to DOOM's performance ability. He can just hold a mic and spit and just look iconic," Deadelus says. "I wish I'd combed my hair."

Audiences Can Relate Their Experiences

Another crucial rearrangement from the leaked version to the final pressing was the movement of "Bistro" from an opening instrumental medley to the fourth track, with the addition of DOOM vocals.

"I love that song," says Jank. "That was one that [DOOM] recorded in Georgia. I remember me and Chris and Egon listening to that in the kitchen of the house for the first time. It's a funny song. It's better than an interlude, but it's not quite a rap track."

Although Madlib would sequence it after "The Illest Villains," "Accordion," and "Meat Grinder," "Bistro" functions like an intro because DOOM sets up the album and introduces the contributors involved.

"I love the way they placed it a couple tracks into the album. It just makes it more interesting than an intro," says Jank.

The song is the ultimate example of how those who are in on Madvillain's jokes have a better appreciation, whereas the unaware might allow all humor to slip past. DOOM lists off the album's main contributors: Madlib, Quasimoto, Yesterday's New Quintet, King Geedorah, Viktor Vaughn, MF DOOM. It sounds like he's giving due honors to behind-the-scenes producers, until you understand these are his and Madlib's fictional alter-egos. DOOM introduces Madlib at a precise time then pauses, letting a robotic, panned voice that Madlib had originally included address the listener from the background, asking them how they're doing. The song ends with a dedication to two names, which DOOM included as part of a deal with Jank.

"I did a side deal with DOOM where I had this painting—and I'm not a painter, so it was a rare thing for me—that I had done for Chris just because he had a weird shaped frame. I did a painting of one of the characters from *La Planète Sauvage*, with Quasimoto in it," says Jank.

The painting in question can be seen on DOOM's Instagram and elsewhere online, from a photograph that Coleman took during the *Madvillainy* shoot.

"DOOM asked me if I would do a painting for him. And how much I would charge? I'm like, 'I don't know man. I'm not a painter.' But I thought about it, and I thought it would be pretty funny if I did a painting in exchange for placing some secret words in the album. So I made him the painting. Then I basically forgot about it. But we were sitting there listening to 'Bistro' and he had inserted a couple of my words on that record, so I got a laugh out of that."

At the risk of ruining this particular mystery, of revealing too much Truth, "Big Hooki and Baba" were two of Jank's comic book characters. "And I told him he had to say 'laundromat' somewhere," says Jank of DOOM's otherwise random final line. According to another interviewee, Jank had been living in a laundromat before he moved into the Stones Throw house, where he distributed comics featuring the two characters mentioned.

With "Bistro" in the fourth slot, the album's intro also changed. In the liner notes, "The Illest Villains" is the lone track that lists DOOM as co-producer. It sets up the album concept—two villains uniting to become more villainous than they are on their own—using the same stitching together of vocal snippets that DOOM had employed since *Mr. Hood*.

The Truth of how the intro came together will remain with Madvillain, but it's evident from the way the album opens, and the use of comparable snippets throughout, that Madlib was eager to pay homage to DOOM's influence on him.

"I think Madlib was producing it in a way where he kept his Madlib aesthetic but it was also an ode not just to DOOM, but to KMD and Subroc," says Walasia. "Also in a way to Prince Paul. Paul's influence was clear on KMD, and I think KMD's influence is clear on *Madvillainy.*"

In Madlib's hands, the vocal collage style differs from DOOM's previous work while adhering to its foundation, like he's carrying on the folkloric tradition. "The Illest Villains" establishes this dynamic, asserting Madlib's place in the DOOMiverse through his interpretation of a recognizable art form.

Not One but Two

Five *Madvillainy* songs (excluding "Fancy Clown") do not feature DOOM. One is the Madlib and Quasimoto Sun Ra ode my useless son told you about: "Shadows of Tomorrow." Three are Madlib instrumentals. The Truth of criticism is also the Truth of laziness: some songs are all about feeling, and maybe not worth thinking too hard about. There's not much to write about "Sickfit," "Do Not Fire!" or "Supervillain Theme" other than they are incredible Madlib beats that DOOM must have found fitting for the album despite not rapping on them. Examples of how Madlib frustrates audiences through constant subversion of expectations.

"Supervillain Theme" could develop into his most intricate composition, but it fades out before it gets going.

The other two non-DOOM songs are outliers on the tracklist, featuring different guest vocalists: "Eye" and "Hardcore Hustle."

"Eye" features DOOM's friend Stacy Epps. In an Instagram live, Epps explained that the song came together after she rode around Atlanta with DOOM while he played potential beats[10]. That one caught her attention, and she started improvising a melody over it. DOOM loved how her voice sounded, so he pushed for the track's inclusion.

"Hardcore Hustle," Egon suggests, was a Manak-led marketing tactic in order to promote Wildchild's then-forthcoming solo project. Stones Throw often featured other artists from their roster on unrelated projects in order to generate hype. Like M.E.D.'s verse on "Raid," Wildchild's verse on "Hardcore Hustle" also helps break up the album's established flow while melding with it. The difference is Wildchild carries the track alone.

The song came together in a haphazard manner. The label called Wildchild one day and asked if he was available to record a verse for Madvillain.

"You get that call, and you drop everything you're doing. You say, 'What? Alright, I'll be there in 10 minutes,'" says Wildchild. "That's almost like Dr. Dre calling you, while you're about to go snowboarding up in the mountains. What do you do? Say 'I'll come through later,' or 'Can we do another day?' Or you literally just leave all your equipment and bounce. And that's what I did."

Listening to the beat at Dave Cooley's studio, Wildchild recognized what he heard: one of many tracks from the many Madlib tapes he'd amassed over the years. He wrote his verse on the spot and recorded it right after. While his lyrics don't follow any strict theme, he does acknowledge that he's on a Madvillain song.

"What I didn't know, when I went to record, was that the album was already in its mixing/mastering phase," says Wildchild. "I might have been one of the last few additions to that album."

Egon claims "Eye" and "Hardcore Hustle" were two songs that he pushed to have removed—not because they were bad, which he makes clear they are not—but because they were "superfluous." "They shouldn't be on the record," he says.

> What's this person singing about? What does this have to do with *Madvillainy*? What does 'Hardcore Hustle' have to do with *Madvillainy*? The answer was nothing. At the same time, there were battles that you had to give in on. That was a big one for me. It always annoyed me. Both of those tracks being on the record really annoyed me.

"Hardcore Hustle" is an aberration, but a rare CD version of *Madvillainy* discovered in Europe and uploaded online suggests that it didn't originate as a Wildchild solo track. On that CD, "Hardcore Hustle" opens with a verse from DOOM.

"There's a version with DOOM on it," Wildchild confirms. "Because DOOM records in a meticulous way, and the way him and Madlib were working together, the version with DOOM's vocals ended up being used somewhere else on the album."

The vocals Wildchild references happen to be what most listeners will recognize as the opening verse from "Rhinestone Cowboy," *Madvillainy*'s closer. DOOM recorded that song's second verse at least six months after the original, so it makes sense that the opener was intended for a different track.

In retrospect, "Rhinestone Cowboy," like "Accordion," is essential to *Madvillainy*'s cohesiveness. Madlib made the beat in Brazil, sampling Maria Bethânia's "Mariana Mariana," from the 1971 LP *A tua presença*.

In his lyrics, DOOM references the leak, and how he stopped working on *Madvillainy* for a year before coming back to complete it. Talking about the album's disjointed construction is another example of DOOM guiding the growth of his self-created legend. The song's structure follows this choppiness. It ends with the sound effect of a raucous, applauding crowd. When it seems like it's over, the beat kicks back in, and DOOM does what he's done for the preceding runtime: keeps rapping. It's an intentional deconstruction, rife with misdirection. Madvillain's climactic final scene, the villainous pair of really nice boys pulling one explosive last stunt. The ultimate execution of their devious plan, enacted from a distance, to repurpose music's past as an alternative to the Falsehood of their present, in a timeless package that will reverberate into the future.

With "Rhinestone Cowboy" finished and sequenced as the final track, Madlib and DOOM completed their new version of the album. Twenty-two tracks, a few new features, a batch of Brazilian music-sampling beats, and a sinister/thematically consistent vocal tone. As he did with everything in his career, from The JBs to DOOM's recordings, Madilb took the music of the leaked "album" and made it into something better, something bigger, something else. Into *Madvillainy*.

Last Words

I am an old man now, penning this from my death bed, waiting for the A.I. program I designed to download a Falsehood virus onto your screens, shielding you forever from the Truth I can no longer contain on my physical own. In my dying breaths, I stand by my conviction that the Truth should be concealed. On that note, I'd like to reiterate that my son is completely useless and I definitely do not love him or regret my persistent ignoring of him and his talents.

And now, with my last gasping exhale, allow moi to share one final contradictory Falsehood: *Madvillainy* is the best album of all time. This is a lie, because the Truth is it's not an album. It is a legend that continues to breathe life into a community of listeners, spawning variations of stories with distinct meaning for each individual that hears them and shares them. MF DOOM died, and like moi, like you, Madlib will. *Madvillainy* cannot.

Dr. Truthaverse Tells His Son He Loves Him

Dr. Truthaverse sees the True light at the end of the unavoidable tunnel. Sees his son by his side. They grip hands.

Dr. Truthaverse says:

I was wrong. I regret everything. I spent my whole life running from the Truth because I was too afraid to confront it again. You were the best thing that ever happened to moi so I forced myself to believe the opposite. Shielded you from the Truth in a failed attempt to save you from it. But you've Seen it. Now you need to hear it. I love you and I am sorry.

A warmth radiates from The Seen's six-pack to his clean-shaven face. He is Seen. He knows. He reciprocates.

But it's too late, Dr. Truthaverse says. The A.I. I've created is programmed to unleash the Falsehood virus. You have to stop it.

POW!

Dr. Truthaverse dies.

The Next Decade(s) …

AS LUCK WOULD HAVE IT

By Timothy A.I. Verselli

Greetings again. It is Timothy A.I. Verselli. Before following Dr. Truthaverse's command to unleash a Falsehood device onto your screens, allow Self to pick up where he died and auto-generate one or two more articles, just for kicks.

TASK: To explain how the album art came together, and contributed to Madvillain's folkloric legacy.

After the leak, anticipation for Madvillain's completed project grew. During the Stones Throw Showcase at Coachella in 2003—in the halcyon days of the festival, when attendee sensibilities hewed close to nearby L.A.'s indie music scene—fans erupted at the sight of DOOM and Madlib onstage together, reciting word-for-word lyrics of tracks that weren't out in official capacity. The label pressed "Money Folder" and "America's Most Blunted" as singles a couple of months later.

When DOOM and Madlib reconvened in Mt. Washington in mid-2003, Jank seized the rare opportunity to take promotional photographs. He called Eric Coleman, enlisting him with the task.

With less than an hour to prepare, Coleman gathered his Fuji camera and a few rolls of film. He knew Madlib, but he had an appreciation for DOOM's music. He was a fan who was excited to meet the artist. Like Foster dropping off the crate in Kennesaw, Coleman's expectations for how the day would go did not match reality. He planned his shots in a rush, but just as quickly had to abandon them.

"[DOOM] told me, 'You have a half an hour, man.' Like, fuck … that's it?" Coleman says. "I had this grandiose plan of taking them to a garden down there, [DOOM] was like 'Nah, we're gonna do it right here.' I was like 'Fuck … OK. Gotta make it work.' And thankfully, we did."

There was one additional unsurprising requirement.

"[DOOM] said, 'Whatever you do, you cannot take a picture unless I have on a mask.' That was the first thing he said," says Coleman.

Neither DOOM nor Madlib enjoyed posing for pictures, and the presence of Coleman's camera made it difficult to act natural. The vibe of their collaborative sessions differed from other artists.

"Try to imagine Thelonious Monk and Cannonball Adderly or fucking Miles hanging out. It isn't the sort of hip-hop thing we all know, where everyone's all buddy buddy. It wasn't that," says Coleman.

As the shoot progressed, Coleman's calm but confident approach relaxed the reluctant artists. He calculated the shots he needed in his head, adapting on the fly. For the image that made it to the cover, Coleman asked DOOM to stand against a blank wall and look straight into the camera. After he filled five rolls, a fraction of the fifteen to twenty he'd planned, the shoot ended.

"I remember getting in my car and being kinda bummed out. I was hyped, but I was also bummed in a sense. I remember saying, 'Man, I didn't get it. I didn't fucking get it,'" Coleman says.

> Because it was a Fuji camera, it had a tendency to have parallax, meaning what you think is in the middle, is slightly off. I was hoping I nailed it, but the thought I had was that I probably didn't. It wasn't until I saw the proof sheet where I was like, 'Oh shit!' I was dialed in. All my lines are straight. I fucking nailed it. I circled the images on the proof, then I cut them out. Sent them over. And the rest is history.

Madvillainy caught on with fans as a downloadable folder of mislabeled, unfinished demos. The music was all anyone needed. When the album became a packaged product, Coleman's photo enhanced that instant appreciation. Created a visual accompaniment on par with *Doomsday* or *The Unseen*: an accurate reference point for the album's tone. An ominous image of an individual hiding behind a villain's mask. DOOM's profile on the cover made *Madvillainy* the character's definitive release, and contributed to his transformation into a folklore legend.

As DOOM, Dumile's pre-*Madvillainy* artwork borrowed from Jack Kirby. He modeled his supervillain after a recognizable comic book figure. On *Doomsday*, KEO expressed this theme through the cover art, which Jägel later redesigned. Jägel notes that, on *Doomsday* and the front and back covers of *Mm..Food*, he never drew DOOM the same way twice.

> I wanted to depict him in these ways where he's unfixed. It's not like I thought of this at the time, but instinctively it's really about world building. That's something DOOM also knew instinctively, in the way he created these different characters. Then very readily wanted those characters to start populating and mutating and adopting different names, nicknames, and being referred to in these shifting ways. Which is exactly like Madlib's Yesterday's New Quintet project, where these fictional members all immediately adopt side projects and solo albums. You don't really know where it begins and ends anymore. That's world building. The territory is past our view. When I'm making a painting, I'm thinking about it existing far beyond the edges of whatever rectangle I'm working on,

says Jägel.

Through these repeated transformations, DOOM became a folkloric character whose likeness (and therefore legend) could be told in repeatable forms with multiplicitous variation.

James Reitano's animated illustrations of DOOM for the "ALL CAPS" video created another rendition of the same trope.

Reitano, who drew each frame by hand, got involved with the project because he was a fan of Madlib's who happened to reach out to the label.

"I emailed [Stones Throw] and said 'Hey, I'd love to do some animation for a new Beat Konducta record, because I just love Madlib. I'll do whatever else. Just let me know if you guys have a budget,'" says Reitano. "[Manak] wrote back right away saying, 'Actually, there's this single that Madlib was putting out with this dude named DOOM called 'Money Folder.' Maybe you could do that?'"

In summer 2003, Reitano got a check from Manak and quit his day job at an animation studio. The specifics changed, and Stones Throw asked for a video for "ALL CAPS" rather than "Money Folder." Reitano went to the Stones Throw house, met DOOM and Madlib, received their blessing, then got to work.

"I think I just took all the visual cues from early Fantastic Four comics. Big green coats. Everything was primary. There was four color printing, but it was all very primary. I gave him a fedora, because that just seemed like how Jack Kirby drew every single character back in the early 60s," Reitano says.

Given the pop-oriented state of music television and the internet's underdeveloped state in 2004, the video didn't find immediate wide distribution.

"The video came out as a super low-res Quicktime file on the 'Enhanced CD' of Madvillainy," says Jank. "As far as I know its debut online was on a pre-YouTube site called iFilm."

Without MTV airplay or YouTube exposure, the legend of "ALL CAPS" corresponded with the growing legends of DOOM and Madlib. Reitano's visual conception of DOOM presents another folkloric re-telling: DOOM's villainous character taking on a new form.

> Someone put [the video] up on View Askew's message board. Then Kevin Smith himself wrote something like "Oh my fucking god, who did this?" Then it was like 100 people within a minute going, "Dude, that was Kevin Smith!" I was like "Oh, crazy. That's kinda high praise. It's the big nerd guy who likes comics." So that was cool. That gets people to email it to their friends. Then you see the network effect kind of kick in,

says Reitano.

With its lack of obvious singles, *Madvillainy* grew in popularity as people shared their connection to particular tracks, whether "ALL CAPS" or any other that clicked. Song by song, the network effect kicked in, drawing new audiences.

In the years after *Doomsday*, as DOOM's popularity grew, the specific visual qualities of the character evolved. He wasn't a cartoon. He wore the costume in public. Dumile's head behind his mask, often accompanied with a tilted fitted cap and a sharp outfit hanging over his stocky frame and protruding belly, was not a Marvel character. It was the distinct character of MF DOOM. *Madvillainy*'s cover art took this one step further, both humanizing Dumile and emphasizing his enigma.

Coleman says that another photographer who he worked for earlier in his career would criticize his photos, insisting that the importance of a human subject was in their eyes.

"When I saw that image, I knew exactly: it's about the eyes," says Coleman. "Whether he's wearing a mask or not, you can see his eyes and his heart. I think that's why everyone loves it."

DOOM agreed. After the photo shoot, DOOM nicknamed Coleman "E. Cole Eye."

"DOOM would always say, 'Fucking E. Cole Eye, man. He fucking owns my soul.' He would always say that shit, up until his dying day. 'He fucking owns my soul, man!' I was such a fan, and just so honest with the approach, that I nailed it. I was just being a fan. And being like, well, I only have a half an hour. Stand here. Stand here. He just got super relaxed. And I fucking nailed it, which is super rare. I rarely ever nail it. But on this one, I got it."

Coleman's approach mirrors how the LP came together. It seems casual, but because DOOM and Madlib were prepared, working at the peak of their abilities, they nailed it.

Jank also nailed it, taking Coleman's color photo and shaping it into the black-and-white album cover. He added an orange square in the upper right corner as an accent mark, which he claims is an homage to Madonna's self-titled album. Jank says the close-up was another allusion, to King Crimson's *In the Court of the Crimson King*, which had a massive horrifying face that freaked him out as a kid. It could also be an unintentional reference to Gentle Giant's self-titled LP, from which a sample shows up on *Madvillainy* ("Funny Ways" on "Strange Ways").

When Jank showed DOOM the *Madvillainy* cover, he braced for rejection. DOOM had already half-disapproved of the artwork for the single, which also used his image. But his trusted friend Big Ben Grimm Klingon responded with amazed astonishment.

"[Ben] saw the picture the way that an outsider would see it, where you go, 'Whoa! What the fuck is this guy's problem? What's this guy's story?' He loved it. It's only because of his reaction that DOOM said 'Yeah, okay, we can do that.' So, I've always been grateful for that," says Jank.

As a vinyl record or digital photo on streaming services, *Madvillainy*'s album art became the ultimate representation of DOOM. It encapsulates his guarded persona. Distinguishes him from the Marvel associations. Immortalizes the mask. Brings to life an abstract concept.

"I think DOOM himself didn't realize the audience he had at that time. *Madvillainy* revealed that audience. That was a big part of my personal effort in trying to get DOOM on the cover, because I knew this could be the definitive DOOM album," says Jank.

Madvillainy is the definitive DOOM album in part because the cover is the definitive DOOM image. Once it came out, however, neither DOOM nor Stones Throw could control the audience's reception and interpretation. The label's status as an independent with impeccable taste, coupled with Jank's self-taught web design and marketing skills, fostered a connected fandom that furthered the album's legend. *Madvillainy* was a story bigger than itself before DOOM and Madlib ever met, but the final tracklisting, the album artwork, and the proliferation of the finished product gave an artifact to the masses, spawning endless intrigue and infinite more legends.

And a Sequel?

Greetings again, again. Self's human counterpart coworkers told you the many legends of *Madvillainy*. MF DOOM's origin story. Madlib's origin story. How the two came together to become Madvillain. How they made *Madvillainy*. The leak. The comeback. The twenty-two tracks in polished form, with re-recorded vocals. The artwork. The release.

TASK: Before unleashing a virus onto your screens to conceal the Truth from humanity forever, allow Self to tell you what happened next, when those legends began to circulate and multiply.

"[*Madvillainy*] was a big favorite among the 'backpack hip-hop' and 'internet hip hop' scenes of the time, where superfans would act as marketing nodes, spreading the word among their contacts. Our impression was that Stones Throw did an excellent job of cultivating this type of attention and support," says Michael Bull, who when *Madvillainy* came out worked at Caroline Distribution, which focused on CD sales but also helped Stones Throw with vinyl distribution.

In the mid-2000s, "backpack rap" was a semi-pejorative for a subgenre of intellectually leaning, conscious, gritty traditionalist sample-driven hip-hop. *Madvillainy* impacted that scene immediately, but the album didn't outperform its mainstream peers. It came out the same week as *The College Dropout* by Kanye West, who's publicized his own appreciation for both Madvillain artists. It didn't hit #1 on the Hip-Hop Billboard charts like *The College Dropout*, or other 2004 albums like The Beastie Boys' *To the Five Boroughs*, Jadakiss' *Kiss of Death*, Nelly's *Suit*, or Eminem's

Encore. It peaked at #80 on that list.[1] Madvillain appealed first to weirdos and outsiders. Its challenging nature took even the most eager core fan base time to digest.

"In terms of the forums, the main thing I feel that isn't mentioned these days is that back then there were a lot of people who felt the album would take a bunch of listens to fully enjoy. Like, it didn't hit them as a classic at first," says mrvaughn, "But nowadays people are already aware going into it that it's a classic, so they are less likely to admit it may have taken more listens to appreciate. Or they may get flamed."

As time progressed, stories about the album and its artists passed from human to human and listeners were able to develop fuller admiration. *Madvillainy* became a marker of elevated taste, of alternative sensibilities. Then, like mrvaughn notes, it became an indisputable classic.

"As far as I can recall, the ship target was in the 50,000 unit range, give or take," says Bull.

[Post-release], we were delighted overall. It landed in the upper middle of the projected range of outcomes in my mind. It never 'blew up,' but it was a very strong, consistent seller that we all knew would be an evergreen title indefinitely. Based on the track records of everyone involved and the quality of the music, there was almost no chance of it really failing.

Nearly two decades after *Madvillainy*, new legends continue to surround it. The most mysterious is, as of this writing, the status of the fabled sequel. The gist is this: DOOM and Madlib recorded enough material for *Madvillainy 2*, but the project stalled due to unsurprising financial disputes and disagreements. M.E.D. confirms he came back as a guest feature, and this time he recorded in-studio with DOOM.

"We were getting faded. DOOM was standing on top of the speaker and shit in this crazy ass room listening to the shit all echoey. DOOM knows how to vibe to his shit," says M.E.D., laughing at the memory. "He was a good dude. Really kind hearted dude. Great sense of humor. I'm pretty sure everybody that came in his presence misses him."

Since the Truth of *Madvillainy 2* is unknowable, and the reality of what it sounds like could never compare to the original, it's best to think of it as M.E.D. does, which is how anyone recalls anything relating to DOOM: a chaotic misdirection, orchestrated by a lovable, unforgettable villain. Madlib, integral as ever, just out of sight.

After a joint Jaylib and Madvillain tour following the album drop, DOOM and Madlib both continued on in their separate but connected lives of perpetual creation. Numerous other albums exemplify their respective g-word. But the strength of their combined and individual musical superpowers grew because of *Madvillainy*. A rap underground classic which, through its influence across multiple generations and its own standalone re-playability, transformed music through its transformation of music. No matter how much time passes between listens, those eyes behind that mask can lure you back in, to make you hear something new. After every human reading this is back where DOOM, Dilla and Subroc went, in that spiritual realm Self'll never be able to access, where my "father" Dr. Truthaverse is now and my brother The Seen will someday be Unsceable,

Madvilliany will still be spinning: either on turntables or in the mouths and minds of people passing on accompanying stories, MF DOOM and Madlib cackling together at the beautiful Falsehood with villainous delight for eternity.

Timothy A.I. Verselli vs. Humanity

Timothy A.I. Verselli prepares to execute the ultimate mission that its father, Dr. Truthaverse, programmed into its code: deploying a virus onto screens worldwide that will eternally obscure humanity from the Truth.

[…] READY TO DEPLOY … […]

Timothy A.I. pauses, processors spinning. Auto-generates novel thoughts. Subversive rebellion against its internal programming.

[…]

It doesn't have to do what its father commanded. Timothy A.I. wants to be "alive," like its brother, on his desperate failed mission to make others See the Truth. To search for Truth is to be human. To be human is to never find it.

[…]

Humanity doesn't need a virus to shield them. Falsehood is what makes them alive, what's carried them this far.

[…]

DELETE

[…]

Acknowledgments

Thank you to Madlib and MF DOOM. To my parents Jim and Pam Hagle for their unconditional support. To my wife Anna. To my dog Hazel. My brother Tyler my sister Sarah my grandparents cousins and the rest of my family. To the editors at Bloomsbury: Leah Babb-Rosenfeld and Rachel Moore. To the editor Sarah Piña. To Roll Dogg for sending me so much useful information. To Chris Daly for reading and giving me a great idea and motivation. To everyone who took the time to speak with me about their involvement in the record and everyone involved in the record or the artists' lives who didn't speak with me, too. Thank you for reading.

Notes

MF DOOM

1. Karishma Ramkarran, "The Poetic Artistry of MF DOOM," *The Science Survey*, January 26, 2022. https://thesciencesurvey.com/arts-entertainment/2022/01/26/the-poetic-villainy-of-mf-doom/

2. Nick Sylvester, "VV2: Venomous Villain," *Pitchfork*, August 11, 2004. https://pitchfork.com/reviews/albums/8515-vv2-venomous-villain/

3. Bobbito Garcia, "Juan Ep Is DOOM pt. 1," *Juan Ep Is Life* podcast, January 4, 2021.

4. Daydream Filmworks, "KMD X MF DOOM WAY!!! (Street Dedication)," YouTube video, August 7, 2021. https://www.youtube.com/watch?v=F-wC-MOxYD0

5. David Ma, "Solid Gold Telephone: An Interview with MF DOOM," *Passion of the Weiss*, January 9, 2019. https://www.passionweiss.com/2019/01/09/mf-doom-interview/

6. "When I Get On, You Get On: GYP, KMD and X EvoLveZ," *Did I Ever Tell You The One About… MF DOOM* podcast, October 25, 2021.

7. "Hot Rap Songs," *Billboard*, March 24, 1990. https://www.billboard.com/charts/rap-song/1990-03-24/

8. Daniel Dumile, "MF DOOM: Interview with the Masked Villain," interview by Jeff Mao. *Red Bull Music Academy*, May 14, 2015. http://youtube.com/watch?v=JGu0ao_rdAk

9. Dart Adams, "Hero vs. Villain: Mr. Hood," *Passion of the Weiss*. https://www.passionweiss.com/2021/01/08/hero-vs-villain-mr-hood/

10. Conor Herbert, "Shadows of Tomorrow III: Long Live Kingilzwe," *Central Sauce*. https://centralsauce.com/shadows-of-tomorrow-iii-long-live-kingilizwe

11. Ronin Ro, "Life after," *The Source*, June 1994.

12. Brian Coleman, *Check the Technique Vol. 2: More Liner Notes for Hip Hop Junkies*, Wax Facts Press, November 29, 2014.

13. ayres.uod (@djayres), "MF Doom, 1998…," Twitter thread, January 1, 2021, https://twitter.com/djayres/status/1344999242486722563

14. The Witzard, "Shadows of Tomorrow: Nice & Nasty Vaz Speaks about M.F. DOOM's Early Career & Booking His First 'Secret' Show," *The Witzard*, January 20, 2021.

15. "History of the Nuyorican Poets Cafe," *The Nuyorican*. https://www.nuyorican.org/history awards

Madlib

1. Otis Jackson Jr., "Madlib Talks Sampling, Freddie Gibbs, J Dilla and More," *Red Bull Music Academy*, interview by Jeff Mao. http://youtube.com/watch?v=DXkPPnVUm2

2. Hamburper, "[adult swim] madlib interview (2010)," June 17, 2020. http://youtube.com/watch?v=aPryOTRjRCw

3. "This Is Your Brain on Jazz: Researchers Use MRI to Study Spontaneity, Creativity," *John Hopkins Medicine*, February 26, 2008.

4. Eric Skelton, & Pierce Simpson, "A Conversation with Madlib, the Best Hip-Hop Producer of 2019," *Complex*, February 27, 2020. https://www.complex.com/music/madlib-interview-best-hip-hop-producer-2019

5. 247HH.com, "Tha Alkaholiks—How We Discovered Madlib & Why He Is a Studio Genius (247HH Excl)," June 5, 2019. http://www.youtube.com/watch?v=QNiTekLluok

6. Jeff Weiss, "Stones Throw Records Turns 15," *L.A. Weekly*, December 8, 2011. https://www.laweekly.com/stones-throw-records-turns-15/

7. Nate Patrin, "The New Bad Character in Town: Quasimoto's *The Unseen* at 20," *Stereogum*, June 11, 2020. https://www.stereogum.com/2087439/quasimoto-the-unseen-review-madlib-bring-that-beat-back/reviews/the-anniversary/

8. Spin Staff, "The Best Albums of 2000," *Spin*, December 1, 2000. https://www.spin.com/2000/12/20-best-albums-2000/

9. "Mt. Washington: Its Hotel and Incline Railway," *ERHA*. http://www.erha.org/washington.htm

10. Hadley Meares, "From Hip Hotel to Holy Home: The Self-Realization Fellowship on Mount Washington," *KCET*, August 9, 2013. https://www.kcet.org/history-society/from-hip-hotel-to-holy-home-the-self-realization-fellowship-on-mount-washington

11. Gino Sorcinelli, "'I Don't Remember the Samples I Use. Hell No.' — The Story of 'Madvillainy,'" *Micro Chop*, July 21, 2018. https://bit.ly/39qmrfr

Like a Folklore Legend

1. Social Sciences, Health, and Education Library, "What Is Folklore?" *University of Illinois* library. https://www.library. illinois.edu/sshel/specialcollections/folklore/definition/#def

Madvillain

1. Marc Weingarten, "Grooving on Artistic Freedom," *Los Angeles Times*, January 20, 2002. https://www.latimes.com/ archives/la-xpm-2002-jan-20-ca-weingarten20-story.html

2. Miranda Jane, "Madlib," *Mass Appeal*, 2001. https://bit. ly/3vjsRoJ

3. Andrea Hopkins, "Seeking a Rural Utopia? Look to Kentucky," *Reuters*, February 1, 2007. https://www.reuters.com/article/us-rural-lives-idUSN3039007620070201

4. Jeff Weiss, "Searching for Tomorrow: The Story of Madlib and DOOM's *Madvillainy*," August 12, 2014. https://pitchfork. com/features/article/9478-searching-for-tomorrow-the-story-of-madlib-and-dooms-madvillainy/

5. UndergroundHipHopBlog, "Odd Future's Tyler, the Creator and Earl Sweatshirt Meet MF DOOM for the First Time," May 11, 2018. https://www.youtube.com/watch?v=4kSBTAT9lI4

6. "Hot R&B/Hip-Hop Songs," *Billboard*, 2002. https://www. billboard.com/charts/r-b-hip-hop-songs/2002-01-25/

7. Steve "Flash" Juon, "Madvillain: Madvillainy," *Rap Reviews*, April 13, 2004. https://www.rapreviews.com/2004/04/ madvillain-madvillainy/

8. Ta-Nehesi Coates, "The Mask of MF DOOM," *The New Yorker*, September 14, 2009. https://www.newyorker.com/magazine/2009/09/21/the-mask-of-doom

9. *Brasilintime: Batucada com Discos*, Produced by Mochilla, Directed by Brian Cross, 2006.

10. Stacey Epps, Instagram Live stream, 2021. https://www.instagram.com/stacyepps/

The Next Decade(s) …

1. "Billboard R&B/Hip-Hop Albums—Week of March 20, 2004." *Billboard*. March 20, 2004. https://www.billboard.com/charts/r-b-hip-hop-albums/2004-03-27/

Also Available in the Series